Dimensions
— of —
NEED

An Atlas of Food and Agriculture

Food and Agriculture Organization of the United Nations
Rome, Italy

This book, issued on the occasion of the 50th Anniversary of the Food and Agriculture Organization
of the United Nations, has been prepared with financial support from:
British Overseas Development Administration
Ministère français des Affaires étrangères
Ministerio español de Agricultura, Pesca y Alimentación
Ministry of Agriculture, Nature Management and Fisheries,
and Ministry of Foreign Affairs, The Netherlands
Italian National Committee for celebration of the 50th Anniversary
of the United Nations

Editor
Tony Loftas

Assistant to the Editor/Principal researcher
Jane Ross

Contributing editors
Geoffrey Lean, Don Hinrichsen, Mary Lean, Christine Graves, Peter Lowrey

Editors
Jane Lyons, Helen de Mattos-Shipley, Felicity Greenland,
Julia Holgate, Anna Sánchez

Principal technical advisers
Tim Aldington, Robert Brinkman, William Clay, Stephen Dembner,
Jacques Du Guerny, Serge Garcia, James Greenfield,
Simon Hocombe, Simon Mack, Jorge Mernies, Franco Pariboni,
Richard Perkins, Wim Sombroek, Jeff Tschirley

Other technical advisers
Abdolreza Abbassian, Nikos Alexandratos, Murthi Annishetty,
Sebastiao Barbosa, Christian Chikhani, Adele Crispoldi-Hotta,
Guido Gryseels, Ali Arslan Gürkan, Klaus Janz, Panos Konandreas,
Andrew Macmillan, Miles Mielke, Berndt Müller-Haye,
Freddy Nachtergaele, Christel Palmberg-Lerche, Paul Reichert,
Ed Rossmiller, Roland Schürmann, Hermann Schmincke,
Jan Slingenbergh, Jerzy Serwinski, Victor Villalobos,
Robin Wellcome, Chan Ling Yap

Many other FAO staff, too numerous to name individually, have also
assisted by virtue of their contributions to the work of the Organization and
advising on specific questions. The editors and compilers of the book have
also received significant assistance from other agencies and organizations
both within and outside the United Nations system including the
International Fund for Agricultural Development (IFAD), the International
Service for National Agricultural Research (ISNAR), the United Nations
Environment Programme (UNEP), the Office of the United Nations High
Commissioner for Refugees (UNHCR), the World Bank, the World Food
Programme (WFP) and the World Health Organization (WHO).

French, Spanish and Italian editions
French: Elizabeth Ganne, Anne Walgenwitz, Ros Schwartz, Myriam Boyden
Spanish: Daniel Nogués Durán, Darío Moreno Falcón
Italian: Ros Schwartz, Manuela Guastella, Luca Salice, Ernestine Shargool

Design
Ian Price

Cartography and diagrams
David Burles

Illustrations
Mikki Rain

FAO graphics and FAO photo research
Scott Grove, Alex Rossi, Nick Rubery, Giampiero Diana,
Giuditta Dolci-Favi, Joanna Maltby-Monaldini, Sergio Pierbattista,
Francesco Sponzilli (stamps, coins and medals)

Colour separations: Fleet Litho
Printed and bound in the UK by the KPC Group, London and Ashford, Kent

No part of this book may be reproduced by any means, or transmitted, or
translated into a machine language without the written permission of the
publisher

The designations employed and the presentation of material in this
publication do not imply the expression of any opinion whatsoever on the
part of the Food and Agriculture Organization of the United Nations
concerning the legal status of any country, territory, city or area or of its
authorities, or concerning the delimitation of its frontiers or boundaries.
The designations "developed" and "developing" are intended for statistical
convenience and do not necessarily express a judgement about the stage
reached by a particular country, territory or area in the development process.

The stamps, coins and medals featured in the book are available through:
Money and Medals Programme, FAO, Rome, Italy

A Banson production
Prepared in cooperation with the Information Division,
Food and Agriculture Organization of the United Nations
by Banson
3 Turville Street, London E2 7HR

First published in 1995 by
the Food and Agriculture Organization of the United Nations
Viale delle Terme di Caracalla, 00100 Rome, Italy
All rights reserved
Reprinted March 1996

Copyright ©1995 by FAO
ISBN 92-5-103737-X

FAO – 50 years on:
A celebration and a challenge

Fifty years ago there were 2 500 million people in the world. Today there are an estimated 5 700 million, and in 50 years' time, there may be 8-10 000 million people to feed, clothe and shelter. Every second, there are three new mouths to feed.

When FAO was founded, the majority of the world's population made their living through agriculture and the exploitation of natural resources. By the turn of the century, the majority will live in cities of the developing world.

The challenge is to meet the needs of humanity now and into the future without permanently damaging our life support system.

In its first 50 years, FAO has much to be proud of. Many people enjoy a better quality of life because of its programmes. However, there is no room for complacency. The needs of increasing populations, poverty, malnutrition, land degradation, deforestation, pollution, loss of biological diversity and the over-exploitation of the oceans remind us that no organization can rest on its laurels. More than 1 000 million people live in poverty which, with rapid population growth, has taken its toll on the environment. No single organization or aid agency can tackle these problems alone.

● We must seek better and sustainable ways and means to meet and overcome these challenges.

● We must reduce waste and improve efficiency in the channels and systems we use.

● We must work in more effective partnerships.

● We must transform agriculture to combine increased productivity with sustainability of natural resources.

As the Minister responsible for the British aid programme, I have been much heartened by recent progress. The new age of democracy in South Africa heralded by the 1994 elections was, without doubt, a highlight. India has achieved remarkable improvements in food security. And during a recent visit I saw how, by providing training and banking credit for destitute women, the Bangladesh Rural Development Committee had enabled nearly half a

> "
> **Awareness and consensus are vital**
> "

The Rt Hon the Baroness Chalker of Wallasey
Minister for Overseas Development
United Kingdom

million women to set up small rural enterprises. These are the kind of successes we must build on.

This book celebrating FAO's 50th Anniversary is about the challenges past, present and future faced by communities in countries like South Africa, India and Bangladesh to improve the quality of their lives. It aims to inform and educate: awareness and consensus are vital tools for alleviating poverty and tackling the problems of the environment. It presents information in a way that is accessible to all. It will, I hope, help a better understanding of the issues and how we might make our world a better place.

The UK is proud to have been one of the countries that founded FAO. Its first Director-General – Lord Boyd Orr – was from Britain. He had helped formulate the policies and programmes which, despite the siege economy of the Second World War, succeeded in doubling agricultural production and improved

nutrition between 1939 and 1945. Since then the UK has played an active part in the evolution and activities of the Organization. British and Commonwealth expertise have made a substantial input into FAO's projects and programmes.

At Rio, the governments of the world agreed that the goal was "sustainable economic and social development" – economic growth and improved quality of life with environmental conservation. FAO has a key role to play. We all have a role to play.

We are giving our own bilateral aid programmes a sharper focus and clearer objectives, and look for similar reforms within FAO and the UN system. We are keen to see the Organization adapt to the changing environment and respond to the membership's priorities and demands.

I am very happy, therefore, that the Overseas Development Administration has been able to help support the preparation of this book.

Contents

Food and people

Protect and produce

CONTENTS

Building the global community

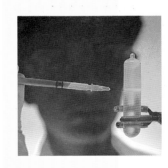

CONTENTS

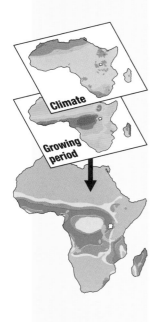

Food and agriculture: The future

Introduction

If understanding leads to compassion, then my fervent hope is that this book will help the reader understand the principal issues involved in feeding the world. It could make a difference to 800 million chronically undernourished people. This book, published on the occasion of FAO's 50th Anniversary, is not about the Organization as such but the challenges that have largely determined its agenda. They can best be summarized in terms of inequality, hunger and poverty.

The Organization that I have the honour to lead is but a single agency within the United Nations system. We are trying our best, with the limited resources made available by the community of nations, to promote improved nutrition and help developing countries produce more food without harming the environment. The issues covered in this book touch billions of people every day of their lives.

FAO plays a unique role: its international team of development specialists tackle food and agricultural problems not only from a global perspective but also at regional and national levels. Since it is at the service of all its member nations, FAO is perfectly placed to act as a neutral forum and to give objective advice to governments. It encourages debate on the important food and agricultural issues described in this book. Thanks to its network of representatives accredited to over 100 member countries, the Organization also keeps abreast of environmental and socio-economic change in every corner of the earth.

How FAO came into being

The origins of FAO can be traced back to the pioneering efforts of the American David Lubin who, in the 1880s, began pressing for a better deal for the world's food producers. He recognized that agriculture was at a disadvantage in comparison with industry, commerce and finance because farmers were not effectively organized. He also realized that international trade played such a role in establishing prices that only a global organization could defend

> **The first cause of hunger and malnutrition is poverty**

Dr Jacques Diouf
Director-General of
the Food and Agriculture
Organization of the
United Nations

farmers' interests satisfactorily. Lubin found a patron in Italy's King Victor Emmanuel III and in 1905 an international meeting adopted the Convention that established the International Institute of Agriculture.

The work of the Institute was essentially technical, but world events led to a change in the initiative for agricultural and socio-economic development. Agriculture was profoundly affected by the post-1929 world depression: nations proved unable to solve the problems created by the collapse in trade and mounting agricultural surpluses. At the same time, nutrition research was revealing more about dietary requirements for health and discovering widespread malnutrition within even the most advanced countries because of the inadequate consumption of milk, vegetables, fruits and other so-called "protective" foods.

The paradox of malnourishment at a time when food surpluses were taxing the stability of agriculture was analysed in a celebrated speech to the League of Nations by Stanley Bruce, a former prime minister of Australia, on the basis of a memorandum prepared by his economic adviser Frank McDougall. Both men were influenced by British nutritionist John Boyd Orr.

The central message of Bruce's address was that the League should simultaneously assess the potential benefits to public health from increased consumption of "protective" foods and the extent to which this might help solve the agricultural crisis. Delegates realized that this was an area where the League might assume a constructive and significant role.

Progress was halted, however, by the outbreak of war and the collapse of the League of Nations. But the idea was not lost. As early as 1941, Franklin D. Roosevelt, President of the United

INTRODUCTION

States, was speaking of the need for a United Nations organization and calling for "freedom from want".

In 1942, Frank McDougall, on a visit to the United States, found a lively interest in preparing for the food problems of the post-war world. As a result, he drafted a second memorandum on the subject of "a United Nations programme for freedom from want of food". McDougall's proposal came to the attention of President Roosevelt and the two men met. McDougall urged that food should be the first economic problem tackled by the United Nations. The following year, President Roosevelt convened the United Nations Conference on Food and Agriculture at Hot Springs, Virginia, from 18 May to 3 June.

Attended by 44 governments, the conference decided to establish a permanent organization in the field of food and agriculture, and set up an Interim Commission for its preparation. The work of this Commission led directly to the meeting that began on 16 October, 1945, in Quebec City and brought FAO into being as the first of the United Nations specialized agencies.

FAO's broad mandate

In the preamble to the Constitution of the fledgling organization, 44 nations signalled their determination "to promote the common welfare". FAO developed new ways to come to grips with this broad mandate. Its first World Food Survey, published the following year, stated categorically that "it is well known that there is much starvation and malnutrition in the world [yet] vague knowledge that this situation exists is not enough; facts and figures are needed if the nations are to attempt to do away with famine and malnutrition".

FAO went on to pioneer systematic data collection and analysis of the world food situation, but information is only one of the many areas in which FAO has led the way in food and agriculture over the past 50 years. The Organization has been active in education and training, rational use of natural resources, environmental protection, participation of small farmers in development planning, the control of plant and animal pests and

diseases, the conservation of genetic diversity and the promotion of sustainable agriculture and rural development.

When FAO was still young, the old colonial empires disintegrated. As the new nations gained independence, they had to make fundamental public policy decisions. Many countries opted to favour industry as the engine of their economies. The city became the symbol of modernity par excellence and the rural exodus began in earnest. Both trends were to have negative consequences for agriculture and food self-sufficiency. FAO's constitutional commitment to "bettering the condition of rural populations" took on greater urgency with the years as demand for food expanded with populations and production fell behind.

The food crisis of the early 1970s showed governments, international organizations and the public that it was vital to have up-to-date information permanently available on the supply prospects of staple foods. Therefore, FAO established the Global Information and Early Warning System (GIEWS) in 1975. This sophisticated instrument has since issued more than 200 alerts on deteriorating food situations. Every day analysts study dozens of indicators which affect food supply. Satellite images and weather station data show how the growing season is progressing in broad areas of the developing world. In an emergency, major aid donors and humanitarian organizations are alerted. Food aid can soon be on its way.

Paving the way to food security

"The first cause of hunger and malnutrition is poverty". So declared the 1943 meeting in Hot Springs. It is still true today. The countries that suffer most from hunger desperately need economic growth with, of course, a more equitable sharing of the benefits. This is why FAO stresses food security, the step beyond food production and supply. Food security is when all people have access to the food they need for an active and healthy life. I believe that the only feasible option for an early and sustainable improvement in food

security is the enhancement of agricultural productivity, particularly in those countries that are both poor and do not produce the food they need. The key to such gains is efficient technology, applied in a sustainable way to the food crops that can make a difference. FAO now has a new strategy called the Special Programme on Food Production for Food Security in Low-Income Food-Deficit Countries. In 1995, there were 86 such countries.

FAO has also launched an Emergency Prevention System for Transboundary Animal and Plant Pests and Diseases (EMPRES). While FAO has recognized competence in both prevention of, and emergency response to, such problems as desert locust, African swine fever, rinderpest and a host of other pests and diseases, we are at the mercy of the processes of alerts and mobilization of resources, which inevitably take time. EMPRES will do much to increase the impact of FAO's actions.

World Agriculture: Towards 2010, FAO's comprehensive analysis of agricultural trends published in 1995, predicts that the percentage of chronically undernourished people in the developing world will drop from today's 20 percent to just over 11 percent. But even these impressive gains will not suffice to guarantee food for all. In 2010, hunger will still afflict an estimated 650 million people in the world, almost as many people as live in the United States and Western Europe combined. Such predictions make FAO's 50th Anniversary an occasion for both celebration and a renewal of our commitment to fight against hunger and poverty. They bring us back to the important issues covered in this anniversary book which I hope will engage and concern all who read it.

Dr Jacques Diouf
Director-General

A BRIEF HISTORY OF FAO

1943 Forty-four governments, meeting in Hot Springs, Virginia, USA, commit themselves to founding a permanent organization for food and agriculture

1945 First session of FAO Conference, Quebec City, Canada, establishes FAO as specialized UN agency
● Sir John Boyd Orr, British nutritionist, is elected first FAO Director-General
● Washington, D.C. is designated temporary site of FAO headquarters
● FAO has 42 members

1946 First *World Food Survey* gives comprehensive picture of world food situation

1947 Norris E. Dodd, US Under Secretary of Agriculture, is elected second FAO Director-General
● FAO Conference agrees to establish FAO Council to keep under review the state of food and agriculture in the world

1948 First area agriculture survey covers Far East and Latin America
● Indo-Pacific Fisheries Commission established – first regional fisheries body to be set up under the aegis of FAO

1949 International Rice Commission set up
● FAO participation in the Expanded Programme of Technical Assistance formally marks the beginning of the Organization's field programme

1950 The first post-war World Census of Agriculture is compiled, covering 65 countries

1951 FAO headquarters moves to Rome

1952 Transfer to FAO of the library of the International Institute of Agriculture – renamed the David Lubin Memorial Library after the man who pioneered the creation of the Institute in 1905
● Second *World Food Survey* finds

average calorie supply per person remaining below pre-war level
● Desert Locust Programme is formally launched

1953 Philip V. Cardon, formerly of US Department of Agriculture, is elected third FAO Director-General

1954 FAO's Committee on Commodity Problems draws up *Guide Lines and Principles of Surplus Disposal*, used ever since by food aid programmes

1955 A plant protection agency is set up in Central America, part of a global network dedicated to preventing pests and diseases spreading through international trade

1956 B.R. Sen, senior Indian diplomat, is elected fourth FAO Director-General

1957 FAO launches a World Seed Campaign in which 79 countries and territories participate, culminating in the World Seed Year of 1961

1958 FAO's first review of agriculture in sub-Saharan Africa finds yields declining because population growth reduces the fallow period in shifting cultivation below that required by the soil to regenerate

1959 Initiation of UN Special Fund operations puts FAO on road to becoming a major world technical aid agency

1960 Freedom from Hunger Campaign is launched to mobilize non-governmental support

1961 FAO and Unesco embark on preparing a Soil Map of the World to bring order to international soil terminology and nomenclature

1962 The FAO/WHO Codex Alimentarius Commission established, in 1961, to

set international food standards becomes operational

1963 UN/FAO World Food Programme created
● Third *World Food Survey*, covering 95 percent of world population, finds 10-15 percent undernourished and up to half suffering from hunger, malnutrition or both

1964 FAO/World Bank Cooperative Programme is established to stimulate investment in agriculture in the developing world

1965 A panel of experts is established to study ways to protect endangered plant genetic resources

1966 UN/FAO World Conference on Land Reform emphasizes the need for an integrated approach

1967 A.H. Boerma, World Food Programme Executive Director, is elected fifth FAO Director-General

1968 First publication by FAO of *Ceres*, a magazine providing worldwide coverage of agricultural development and issues

1969 FAO releases *Indicative World Plan for Agricultural Development*, an analysis of major issues for world agriculture in the 1970s and 1980s

1970 Second World Food Congress, The Hague, calls on governments to increase resources for development and to channel a greater proportion through international agencies

1971 Consultative Group on International Agricultural Research (CGIAR) is created

1972 UN Conference on the Human Environment, Stockholm, asks FAO to act to conserve the earth's agricultural, forestry, fishery and other natural resources

A BRIEF HISTORY OF FAO

1973 Office for the Sahelian Relief Operation (OSRO) is established to coordinate emergency aid to famine victims in the Sahelian zone of Africa

1974 UN World Food Conference in Rome recommends the adoption of an International Undertaking on World Food Security

1975 Edouard Saouma, Director of FAO's Land and Water Division, is elected FAO's sixth Director-General
● FAO Conference establishes Committee on World Food Security
● FAO has 136 members

1976 Technical Cooperation Programme, financed from FAO funds, is established to provide greater flexibility in responding to urgent situations
● Formal launch of the Food Security Assistance Scheme (FSAS), designed to help developing countries formulate national food security policies

1977 The Global Information and Early Warning System (GIEWS) becomes fully operational

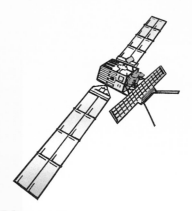

1978 Fourth *World Food Survey* shows that about 455 million people are undernourished in the developing world
● FAO Locust Control Programme responds to a locust plague devastating parts of Africa, the Near East and South-West Asia

1979 World Conference on Agrarian Reform and Rural Development (WCARRD), meeting in Rome, adopts "Peasants' Charter"
● *Agriculture: Toward 2000* is published, providing a prognosis for food and agricultural production over the following two decades

● Plan of Action for World Food Security, adopted by FAO's Council, calls for a voluntary system of nationally held and internationally coordinated food stocks

1980 First session of the FAO Commission on African Animal Trypanosomiasis
● FAO concludes 56 agreements for the appointment of FAO Representatives in developing member countries

1981 The first World Food Day is celebrated on 16 October by over 150 countries

1982 International Seed Information System is inaugurated and a new associated seed laboratory sends out 20 000 seed samples during the year

1983 FAO Council endorses cooperative action for plant health to develop techniques, such as integrated pest control, suitable for smallholders and poor farmers
● Forest Resources Information System (FORIS), containing computerized data on the world's tropical forests, becomes operational

1984 World Conference on Fisheries Management and Development, held in Rome, provides first major follow-up to the new regime for the world's oceans

1985 Fifth World Food Survey is published
● FAO Conference approves a World Food Security Compact, which outlines a plan for achieving a comprehensive food security system
● FAO has 158 members

1986 AGROSTAT, the world's most comprehensive source of agricultural information and statistics, becomes operational
● Pan-African Rinderpest Campaign is launched, operating in 34 countries

1987 FAO recommends safe levels for radioactive contamination of food in international trade

1988 The Africa Real-Time Environmental Monitoring System (ARTEMIS) is installed at FAO headquarters to process satellite data on rainfall and vegetation

1989 FAO Commission on Plant Genetic Resources recognizes right of farmers in the developing world to compensation for use of indigenous germplasm in plant breeding

1990 FAO Regional Conference for Africa adopts the International Scheme for the Conservation and Rehabilitation of African Lands
● FAO reports to the UN Secretary-General on the effect on marine resources of large-scale driftnet fishing

1991 FAO/Netherlands Conference on Agriculture and the Environment at 's-Hertogenbosch, the Netherlands, discussed requirements for sustainable agriculture and rural development as a precursor to the United Nations Conference on Environment and Development (UNCED)
● International Plant Protection Convention is ratified with 92 signatories
● FAO's Screwworm Emergency Centre for North Africa completes a successful campaign to eradicate the pest in Libya

1992 UNCED in Rio de Janeiro, Brazil
● FAO and WHO hold International Conference on Nutrition in Rome which approves a World Declaration and Plan of Action on Nutrition

1993 Dr Jacques Diouf is elected the seventh Director-General of FAO
● FAO Conference reviews *Agriculture: Towards 2010*, which states that despite an increase in food production and food security there are still 800 million undernourished people in the world

1994 Director-General Dr Jacques Diouf restructures FAO to support shifts in priorities such as progressive decentralization of staff away from headquarters and a special programme to grow more staple crops in low-income food-deficit countries

1995 FAO is 50 years old
● A 50th Anniversary International Symposium is held in Quebec City, Canada, followed by a special Ministerial Meeting on food security
● FAO has 171 members

Food and People

Dimensions of Need

Human nutrition: Key to health and development

REPUBLIQUE POPULAIRE DU CONGO
150f
POSTES 1981
JOURNEE MONDIALE DE L'ALIMENTATION
DELRIEU
E MOKOKO

The right to an adequate diet is as fundamental as the right to life itself. World Food Day, on 16 October every year, is a symbolic reminder of this right.

To be healthy and active, our diet (what we regularly eat and drink) must be adequate in quantity and variety to meet our energy and nutrient needs. Most foods contain many different nutrients; no single food, except breast-milk, provides all the nutrients required. The best way, therefore, to ensure the body gets all the necessary nutrients is to eat a variety of foods.

Nutrients are classified as carbohydrates, fats, proteins, vitamins or minerals. Water and dietary fibre are also essential. Each nutrient has specific functions and is made available to the body tissues through the processes of digestion and absorption.

How well foods are digested and their nutrients absorbed can be influenced in several ways. For example, infections, particularly those that accelerate the passage of food through the digestive system, can reduce the body's capacity to absorb nutrients and accelerate the loss of water and body salts. The combination of foods eaten can also affect digestion and absorption. Iron from animal sources is usually well absorbed, but iron in plants is generally not, because of the presence of natural compounds, such as phytates in cereals and tannins in tea, that inhibit iron absorption. Other factors, such as an increased vitamin C intake,

can enhance the absorption of iron from plant sources. Excessive dietary fibre can interfere with the absorption of some nutrients.

Nutrient requirements vary between individuals according to, for example, age, gender, level of activity and health. The ways in which people meet these requirements also vary. There is no ideal or universal dietary pattern and the body is wonderfully adaptive. From arctic tundra to tropical forest, and from big cities to remote islands, various populations demonstrate that human nutritional needs can be met by diverse ranges of foodstuffs and dietary habits.

Pregnant women and nursing mothers need a higher calorie intake than others in their age group to provide for their babies.

What is a balanced diet?

The Food Guide Pyramid is one example of a national food guide. Prepared for consumers in the United States, the pyramid shows the recommended proportions of the various categories of food. It is easy to see that for most Americans, the daily food intake should include a high proportion of cereals, fruits and vegetables whereas fats, oils and sweets are best eaten in moderation.

Nutritional requirements vary from person to person. Everyone needs to pay attention to the quality, quantity and diversity of food sources to have a balanced diet. Many countries have set or suggest dietary guidelines to help people meet their nutritional needs. Since there is no ideal dietary pattern suitable for all people, these guidelines must be developed with a specific food supply and population in mind.

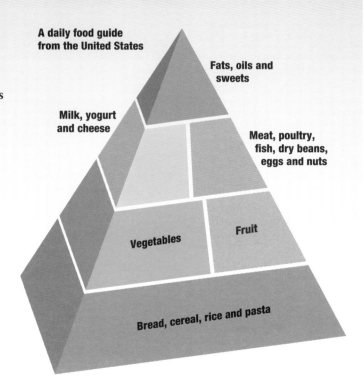

A daily food guide from the United States

Fats, oils and sweets

Milk, yogurt and cheese

Meat, poultry, fish, dry beans, eggs and nuts

Vegetables

Fruit

Bread, cereal, rice and pasta

Food provides us with the energy and nutrients needed for a healthy life.

Nutrients and where to find them

Carbohydrates are the basic source of energy. They range in complexity from simple sugars to complex starches. Sugars are found in sweet foods such as honey, and in milk and fruits. Major sources of starches include cereals, root vegetables, pulses (beans, lentils, peas) and some fruits such as plantains and bananas.

Dietary fats and oils are rich sources of energy and provide essential fatty acids. They can be obtained from both animals and plants. Animal sources include fatty meats, poultry such as duck and goose, butter, ghee and oily fish. Plant sources include oilseeds (sunflower, safflower, sesame), nuts and legumes (peanuts, soybeans).

Proteins, which are long chains of amino acids, form much of the basic structural material of the body; they are necessary for its growth, functioning and repair. The body can make many amino acids but some, called essential amino acids, must be obtained from food. Different foods contain varying quantities of these. Animal products are a prime source, but a mixture of vegetable sources can also satisfy the body's needs. Rich sources of proteins include meat, fish, dairy products, pulses, nuts and cereals.

Vitamins are essential to practically all the body's chemical processes and for maintaining the health and integrity of body tissue. They are usually required in small quantities, but must be consumed regularly because many are not stored well in the body. Vitamin A is found only in animal products, particularly liver, eggs and milk, but many fruits and vegetables such as carrots, mangoes and papaya contain carotenes, chemicals that the body can convert into vitamin A. Good sources of vitamin C are fruits and vegetables. The B complex is found in cereals, legumes, meat, poultry and dairy products.

Minerals are essential to structures such as bones and teeth (calcium) and processes such as energy transfer (iron) and functioning of the body and brain (iodine). We need comparatively large amounts of some minerals, such as calcium – found in peas and beans, milk, meat and cheese – and much smaller amounts of others, such as iron – found in meat, fish and shellfish, dark green leafy vegetables and nuts.

Because vitamins and minerals are usually needed in only small quantities they are called micronutrients.

Energy expenditure

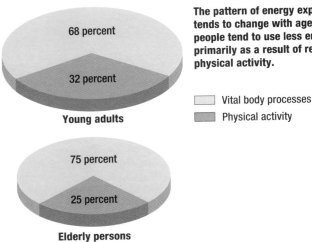

68 percent

32 percent

Young adults

75 percent

25 percent

Elderly persons

The pattern of energy expenditure tends to change with age. Elderly people tend to use less energy, primarily as a result of reduced physical activity.

☐ Vital body processes
☐ Physical activity

Energy requirements

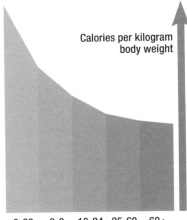

Calories per kilogram body weight

| 0-23 months | 2-9 years | 10-24 years | 25-60 years | 60+ years |

Energy requirements are determined by body size, activity level and physiological conditions such as illness, infection, pregnancy and lactation. As body size increases, so does the total energy requirement; however, per body unit, the energy requirement decreases.

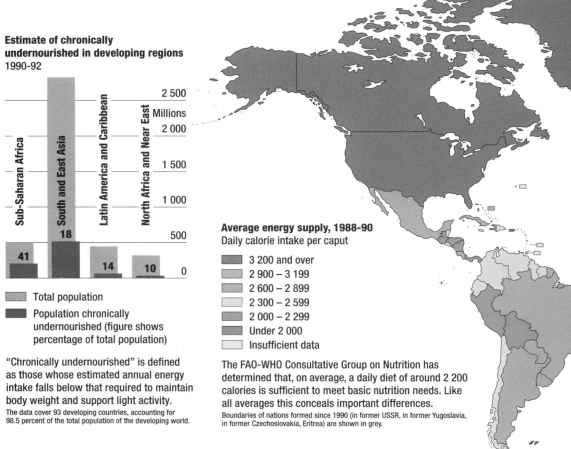

Estimate of chronically undernourished in developing regions 1990-92

Sub-Saharan Africa — 41
South and East Asia — 18
Latin America and Caribbean — 14
North Africa and Near East — 10

Millions: 2 500 / 2 000 / 1 500 / 1 000 / 500 / 0

- Total population
- Population chronically undernourished (figure shows percentage of total population)

"Chronically undernourished" is defined as those whose estimated annual energy intake falls below that required to maintain body weight and support light activity.
The data cover 93 developing countries, accounting for 98.5 percent of the total population of the developing world.

Average energy supply, 1988-90
Daily calorie intake per caput

- 3 200 and over
- 2 900 – 3 199
- 2 600 – 2 899
- 2 300 – 2 599
- 2 000 – 2 299
- Under 2 000
- Insufficient data

The FAO-WHO Consultative Group on Nutrition has determined that, on average, a daily diet of around 2 200 calories is sufficient to meet basic nutrition needs. Like all averages this conceals important differences.
Boundaries of nations formed since 1990 (in former USSR, in former Yugoslavia, in former Czechoslovakia, Eritrea) are shown in grey.

Undernourishment and malnutrition

Over 800 million people, mostly in the developing world, are chronically undernourished, eating too little to meet minimal energy requirements. Millions more suffer acute malnutrition during transitory or seasonal food insecurity. Over 200 million children suffer from protein-energy malnutrition (PEM) and each year nearly 13 million under fives die as a direct or indirect result of hunger and malnutrition.

Malnutrition usually results from diets lacking specific nutrients but can also be caused by so-called "diets of excess".

PEM is most common among young children and pregnant women in the developing world. It is usually caused by energy-deficient diets (that may also lack protein) coupled with infections that raise nutrient requirements while limiting the intake and utilization of food. It is the prime cause of low birth weight and poor growth in the developing world where mothers themselves may have a legacy of low birth weight, stunted growth and anaemia.

Malnutrition can have serious effects, right from conception. Vitamin A deficiency is associated with increased child mortality, and is a prime cause of child blindness. Iodine deficiency leads to slow growth and mental development and to goitre. Anaemia, largely due to iron deficiency, is the most widespread nutritional problem, affecting 2 000 million worldwide. It can impede learning and productivity and is a leading cause of maternal mortality in developing countries. Calcium deficiency is a leading risk factor for osteoporosis, a condition where bones become fragile and brittle. Inadequate vitamin C can lead to scurvy and has been linked to poor absorption of iron and an increased risk of certain non-communicable diseases.

FAO projects to combat undernourishment and malnutrition: training nutrition agents, Lesotho (top); children tending their school vegetable garden, Ecuador (bottom).

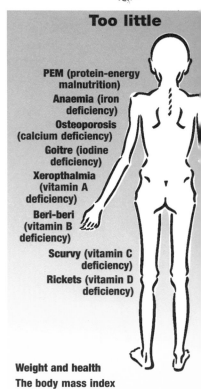

Too little

PEM (protein-energy malnutrition)
Anaemia (iron deficiency)
Osteoporosis (calcium deficiency)
Goitre (iodine deficiency)
Xeropthalmia (vitamin A deficiency)
Beri-beri (vitamin B deficiency)
Scurvy (vitamin C deficiency)
Rickets (vitamin D deficiency)

Weight and health

The body mass index (BMI) gives an easy guide to what body weight is compatible with good health. is calculated by dividing body mass (w in kilograms) by the square of the pers

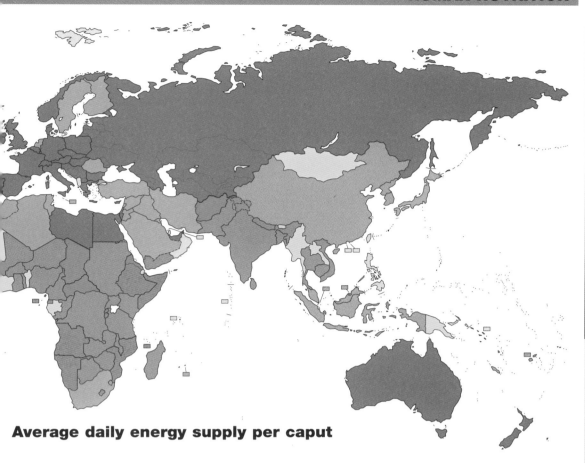

Average daily energy supply per caput

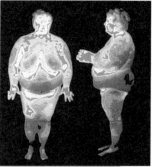

Malnutrition is caused by bad diet as well as lack of food.

Too much

Stroke
Heart/arterial disease
Some cancers
Obesity
Diabetes mellitus
Gallstones
Dental caries
Gout

in metres. In adults the BMI should ween 18.5 and 25. Up to 30 is ered overweight. Values above 30 e obesity.

Diet-related non-communicable diseases

Non-communicable diseases such as cardiovascular ailments, cancer, stroke, hypertension and diabetes have become more common since advances in medicine have reduced the impact of infectious diseases and life expectancy has increased. In the developing world, infectious diseases remain the prime cause of death, but deaths related to diet, activity and lifestyle are on the increase. In the developed world, by far the most common causes of death are non-communicable diseases.

Foremost among factors which contribute to the greater incidence of these diseases is the widespread change towards increasingly sedentary lifestyles. This, combined with dietary change (more fat, less fruit, vegetables and whole grains), can contribute to a wide range of chronic diseases that often lead to permanent disability and premature death.

The relationship between dietary intake, exercise and heart disease is specially strong. Studies show a clear connection between diets extremely high in fats, especially animal fats, and low in fruits and vegetables and an increased risk of obstruction of blood flow and hardening of the walls of the arteries. With the arteries constricted, the heart must work harder to pump blood through them. This extra stress often results in coronary heart disease.

Studies also indicate a direct relationship between diets rich in complex carbohydrates and fibre and a reduced risk of cardiovascular disease and certain cancers, particularly of the lower bowel. Eating fibre-rich foods assists bowel function.

For a healthy lifestyle: avoid tobacco, do not exceed a moderate alcohol intake and take exercise – sufficient to raise heartbeat – for 20 minutes, three to five times a week.

More than 800 million people, over 13 percent of the world's population, do not get enough to eat.

People and populations at risk

Poverty and hunger frequently go together. This Brazilian family has only a small tent to sleep in. All their other activities, including cooking and eating, are done outside.

In the world as a whole, an average of about 2 700 calories of food is available per person per day – enough to meet everyone's energy requirements. But food is neither produced nor distributed equally. Some countries produce more food than others, while distribution systems and family incomes determine access to food. An FAO survey in the mid-1980s discovered that average diets in many of the poorest countries were 2 100 calories a day.

Poor health greatly increases the risk of malnutrition. Infection can increase the body's requirements for energy and various nutrients, but limit the consumption of food and the absorption of nutrients.

In recent decades, health and nutritional status have improved considerably, but are still far from satisfactory in many countries.

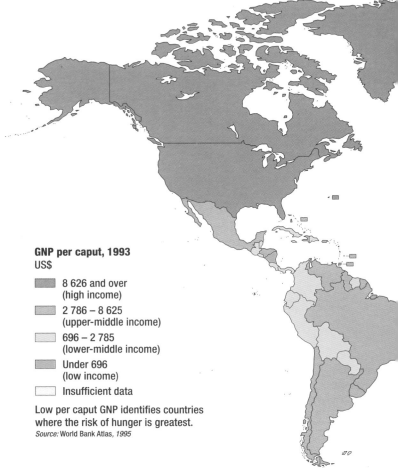

GNP per caput, 1993
US$

- 8 626 and over (high income)
- 2 786 – 8 625 (upper-middle income)
- 696 – 2 785 (lower-middle income)
- Under 696 (low income)
- Insufficient data

Low per caput GNP identifies countries where the risk of hunger is greatest.
Source: World Bank Atlas, *1995*

Rural and urban poor

Poverty is a prime cause of hunger and malnutrition. In many rural areas, protein-energy malnutrition and micronutrient deficiencies are most common among the landless poor and such isolated groups as pastoral nomads and small fishing communities. Inefficient production and lack of access to credit, seeds, fertilizers, extension services and marketing channels can all limit food production.

The rural poor often go hungry in the period just before harvest time when food is scarce. The urban poor are less likely to starve, but inadequate diets, unhealthy lifestyles and overcrowded, unsanitary living conditions make them prone to infection and all forms of malnutrition.

Drought and flood-prone populations

People in drought-prone areas live under a continuous threat of hunger and malnutrition. Droughts in Africa during the 1980s forced 10 million farmers to abandon their land; over 1 million died. The impact of the drought was exaggerated in Ethiopia by government policies which reduced the reserves of food grains held on farms. The cost in lives would have been far greater but for the mobilization of food aid by the international community.

Worldwide, the population affected by floods rose from 5.2 million in the 1960s to 15.4 million in the 1970s. The developing world is particularly affected; in India alone deaths from floods were 14 times greater in the 1980s than the 1950s and the area affected grew from 25 to 40 million hectares.

Rural-urban poverty indicators
Percentages of rural and urban populations living in absolute poverty or lacking access to essential services in the 45 least-developed countries

- Rural
- Urban

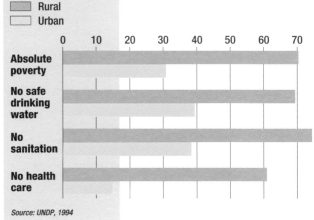

	0	10	20	30	40	50	60	70
Absolute poverty								
No safe drinking water								
No sanitation								
No health care								

Source: UNDP, 1994

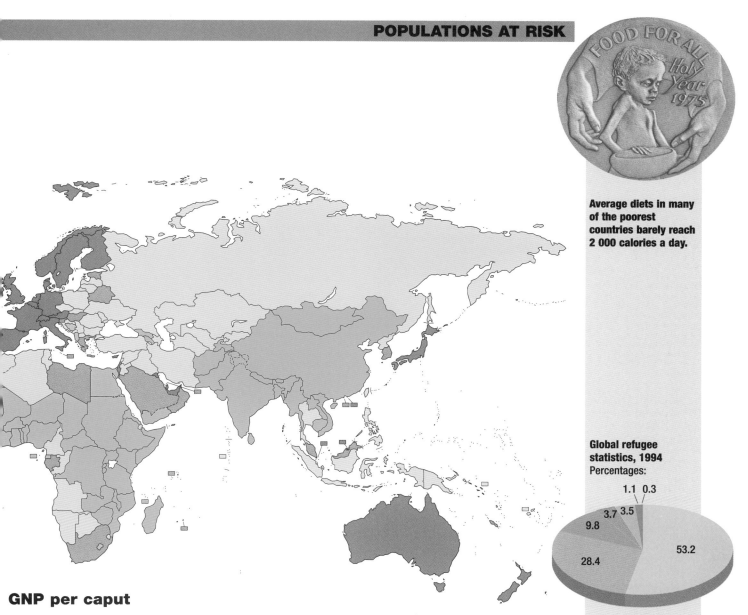

Average diets in many of the poorest countries barely reach 2 000 calories a day.

Global refugee statistics, 1994
Percentages:

1.1 0.3
3.7 3.5
9.8
28.4
53.2

Actual numbers:

- Africa (9 854 200)
- Asia (5 259 900)
- Europe (1 819 200)
- North America (681 400)
- Area of the former USSR (647 500)
- Latin America (196 400)
- Southwest Pacific (51 200)

Total number of concern to UNHCR: 27.5 million; including 18.5 million refugees, 5.5 million internally displaced persons, and 3.5 million others.
Source: UNHCR

GNP per caput

Refugees
There are now over 24 million refugees and displaced persons globally. They often receive just enough food to live, and their diets often lack the micronutrients needed to prevent debilitating diseases such as scurvy and beri-beri.

Women
Many women work longer hours than men but, because of their status, receive less food. Girls may be underprivileged from birth and destined for a heavy work load, poor diet, early marriage and many closely spaced pregnancies. Anaemia is particularly common among women. Malnourished women are likely to have low birth-weight babies, many of whom die in infancy.

Children
Poor families' children may be at risk from a host of debilitating or fatal diseases brought on by unsanitary conditions and inadequate care and feeding. Infection can push children from a state of marginal undernourishment to one of acute malnutrition. The children may also have to work long hours at menial jobs to supplement the family's meagre income, further endangering their development, education and health.

The elderly
People who are old and infirm are increasingly at risk as populations age in developed countries and longevity, but not necessarily health, improves in the developing world. The breakdown of the extended family system and the absence of social services often leave them without care or support.

AIDS sufferers
In the developing world, where AIDS affects men and women equally, the syndrome reduces people's capacity to produce or obtain food and the ability of parents to care for their children. Children of parents with HIV may be infected in the womb and die young, while those spared infection are destined to join the world's 30 million or so orphans.

Africa in context

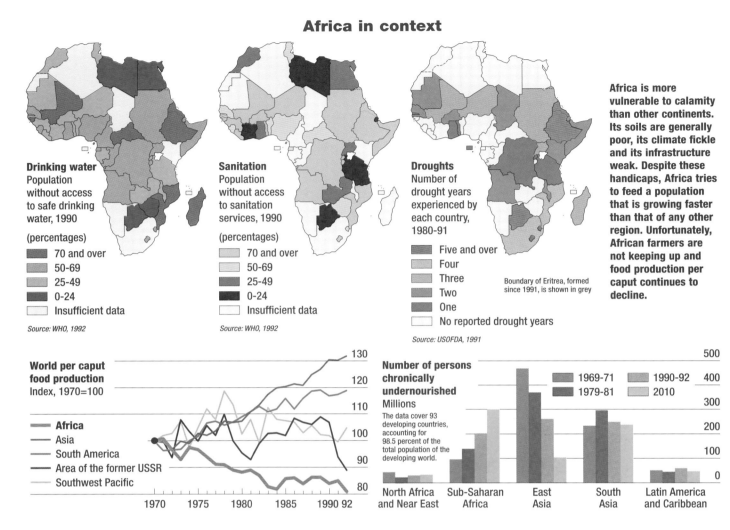

Drinking water
Population without access to safe drinking water, 1990

(percentages)

- 70 and over
- 50-69
- 25-49
- 0-24
- Insufficient data

Source: WHO, 1992

Sanitation
Population without access to sanitation services, 1990

(percentages)

- 70 and over
- 50-69
- 25-49
- 0-24
- Insufficient data

Source: WHO, 1992

Droughts
Number of drought years experienced by each country, 1980-91

- Five and over
- Four
- Three
- Two
- One
- No reported drought years

Boundary of Eritrea, formed since 1991, is shown in grey

Source: USOFDA, 1991

Africa is more vulnerable to calamity than other continents. Its soils are generally poor, its climate fickle and its infrastructure weak. Despite these handicaps, Africa tries to feed a population that is growing faster than that of any other region. Unfortunately, African farmers are not keeping up and food production per caput continues to decline.

World per caput food production
Index, 1970=100

- Africa
- Asia
- South America
- Area of the former USSR
- Southwest Pacific

1970 1975 1980 1985 1990 92

130
120
110
100
90
80

Number of persons chronically undernourished
Millions

The data cover 93 developing countries, accounting for 98.5 percent of the total population of the developing world.

- 1969-71
- 1979-81
- 1990-92
- 2010

500
400
300
200
100
0

North Africa and Near East | Sub-Saharan Africa | East Asia | South Asia | Latin America and Caribbean

The spectre of famine

Famines have afflicted humanity since the dawn of time: the earliest known written record dates from Egypt in 3500 BC. Two famines swept over India in 1702-04 and 1769-70, together killing 5 million people. The worst famine on record in 1876-79 claimed between 9 and 13 million lives in China.

Famines are caused by human factors such as war, and ethnic, religious and tribal conflicts, as well as by adverse weather and other natural hazards, including volcanic eruptions and earthquakes. Poor people are generally much more vulnerable to such disasters than the rich, and are much less able to respond to them.

Little progress has been made in preventing the causes of famine – the number of major disasters increased four-fold between the 1960s and 1980s – but the international donor community has become better at preventing them turning into catastrophes. Between 1980 and 1985, for example, drought, aggravated by widespread land degradation, affected 21 countries and around 150 million people in Africa: but a US$ 1 000 million emergency aid programme coordinated by the United Nations and its agencies saved millions of lives.

Most developing countries now have plans to cope with natural emergencies. Bangladesh, for instance, has an elaborate early warning system for tracking cyclones arriving in the Bay of Bengal.

It has also set up emergency cyclone shelters and food distribution centres.

Some communities are also taking effective preventative action. After a series of devastating droughts in the 1980s, the community of Kibwezi in Kenya, helped by the African Medical and Research Foundation, introduced drought-resistant crops, increased the number of farmed rabbits and domestic fowl, set up tree nurseries and developed energy-saving stoves. Water tanks were constructed and women's groups were helped to initiate and manage activities to generate income. Droughts still threaten the land, but the people of Kibwezi are now better able to cope with them.

Between 1980 and 1985, drought affected around 150 million people in Africa. This nomad waits for an air-drop of food aid in drought-stricken Chad.

Availability of food:
How countries compare

People often go hungry even though food is available because they are too poor to buy it. In the 1943 Bengal famine 2-3 million died, although there was no overall food shortage, because an economic boom raised prices beyond the reach of the poor.

Most of the world's poor and undernourished live in 86 countries that cannot produce enough food to feed their populations and lack the financial resources to make up the deficit through imports.

FAO places special emphasis on improving food production and availability in these low-income food-deficit countries. It is helping farmers in high-potential areas to increase food supplies through sustainable but intensive agriculture. At the same time, subsistence cultivators in areas with poor soil or unreliable rainfall are being encouraged to diversify so as to increase self-reliance and protect the environment.

Twenty-five years ago, 41 percent of the people of East Asia were hungry; by 1992 this proportion had fallen to 16 percent, despite an increase in population of over 500 million. Over the same period the proportion malnourished in Latin America dropped from 18 percent to 14 percent, and in the Near East from 25 percent to 10 percent. Food availability in Africa has improved recently, but the average intake of little more than 2 000 calories a day indicates that many people still receive less than that.

Over the past 25 years, the proportion of chronically undernourished people has declined.

Low-income food-deficit countries, 1995

Latin America and Caribbean
Bolivia
Colombia
Dominican Republic
Ecuador
El Salvador
Guatemala
Haiti
Honduras
Nicaragua

Southwest Pacific
Kiribati
Papua New Guinea
Samoa
Solomon Islands
Tuvalu
Vanuatu

North Africa and Near East
Afghanistan	Jordan	Syrian Arab Republic
Egypt	Morocco	Yemen

Sub-Saharan Africa
Angola	Ethiopia	Nigeria
Benin	Gambia	Rwanda
Burkina Faso	Ghana	Sao Tome and Principe
Burundi	Guinea	Senegal
Cameroon	Guinea-Bissau	Sierra Leone
Cape Verde	Kenya	Somalia
Central African Rep.	Lesotho	Sudan
Chad	Liberia	Swaziland
Comoros	Madagascar	Tanzania, United Rep.
Congo	Malawi	Togo
Côte d'Ivoire	Mali	Uganda
Djibouti	Mauritania	Zaire
Equatorial Guinea	Mozambique	Zambia
Eritrea	Niger	Zimbabwe

Far East
Bangladesh	Maldives
Bhutan	Mongolia
Cambodia	Nepal
China	Pakistan
India	Philippines
Indonesia	Sri Lanka
Laos	

Europe and area of the former USSR
Albania	Tajikistan
Armenia	Turkmenistan
Azerbaijan	Uzbekistan
Georgia	
Kyrgyzstan	
Moldova, Rep. of	
Macedonia, Former Yugoslav Republic of	

Foodcrops and shortages

The world is faced with starvation in the midst of plenty. The majority of the world's poor and undernourished people live in 86 low-income food-deficit countries (LIFDCs). Both Kiribati and Honduras fall into this category and are dependent on food aid. Their stamps shown above commemorate the International Conference on Nutrition in 1992.

Summary forecasts (July/August 1994)

Unfavourable prospects for crops

Food supply shortfall in marketing year requiring exceptional assistance

The Foodcrops and Shortages Special Reports – issued by FAO's Global Information and Early Warning System on Food and Agriculture (GIEWS) – provide up-to-date accounts, country by country, of crop conditions, production prospects and the national food supply situation in both developing and developed countries. Reports specify those countries with severe food shortages and identify those where current crop conditions give cause for concern.

Summary forecasts (September/October 1994)

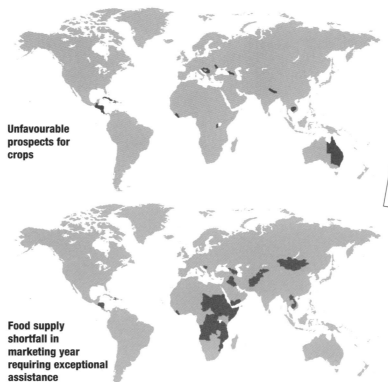

Unfavourable prospects for crops

Food supply shortfall in marketing year requiring exceptional assistance

Staple foods: What do people eat?

The world has over 50 000 edible plants. Just three of them, rice, maize and wheat, provide 60 percent of the world's food energy intake.

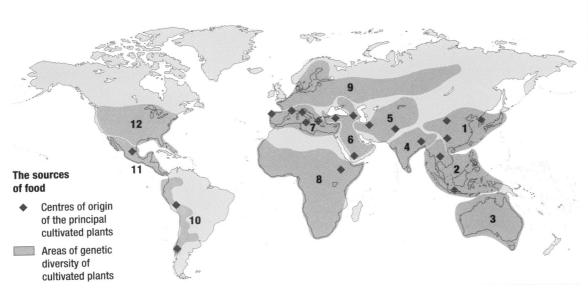

The sources of food

◆ Centres of origin of the principal cultivated plants

▨ Areas of genetic diversity of cultivated plants

Selected food crops:

1. Chinese-Japanese region
bamboo, **millet**, mustard, orange, peach, **rice**, **soybean**, tea

2. Indochinese-Indonesian region
bamboo, banana, coconut, grapefruit, mango, **rice**, sugar cane, **yam**

3. Australian region
macadamia nut

4. Hindustani region
banana, bean, chick-pea, citrus, cucumber, eggplant, mango, mustard, **rice**, sugar cane

5. Central Asian region
apple, apricot, bean, carrot, grape, melon, onion, pea, pear, plum, **rye**, spinach, walnut, **wheat**

6. Near Eastern region
almond, **barley**, fig, grape, **lentil**, melon, pea, pistachio, **rye**, **wheat**

7. Mediterranean region
beetroot, cabbage, celery, fava bean, grape, lettuce, **oats**, olive, radish, **wheat**

8. African region
coffee, **millet**, oil palm, okra, **sorghum**, **teff**, **wheat**, **yam**

9. European-Siberian region
apple, cherry, chicory, hops, lettuce, pear

10. South American region
cacao, **cassava**, groundnut, lima bean, papaya, pineapple, **potato**, squash, **sweet potato**, tomato

11. Central American and Mexican region
french bean, **maize**, pepper/chilli, **potato**, squash

12. North American region
blueberry, sunflower

Staple crops are shown in bold type

A staple food is one that is eaten regularly and in such quantities as to constitute the dominant part of the diet and supply a major proportion of energy and nutrient needs.

A staple food does not meet a population's total nutritional needs: a variety of foods is required. This is particularly the case for children and other nutritionally vulnerable groups.

Typically, staple foods are well adapted to the growth conditions in their source areas. For example, they may be tolerant of drought, pests or soils low in nutrients. Farmers often rely on staple crops to reduce risk and increase the resilience of their agricultural systems.

Most people live on a diet based on one or more of the following staples: rice, wheat, maize (corn), millet, sorghum, roots and tubers (potatoes, cassava, yams and taro), and animal products such as meat, milk, eggs, cheese and fish.

Of more than 50 000 edible plant species in the world, only a few hundred contribute significantly to food supplies. Just 15 crop plants provide 90 percent of the world's food energy intake, with three – rice, maize and wheat – making up two-thirds of this. These three are the staples of over 4 000 million people.

Although there are over 10 000 species in the Gramineae (cereal) family, few have been widely introduced into cultivation over the past 2 000 years. Rice feeds almost half of humanity. Per caput rice consumption has generally remained stable, or risen slightly since the 1960s. It has declined in recent years in many of the wealthier rice-consuming countries,

SIERRA LEONE

The main staple foods in the average African diet are (in terms of energy) cereals (46 percent), roots and tubers (20 percent) and animal products (7 percent).

In Western Europe the main staple foods in the average diet are (in terms of energy) animal products (33 percent), cereals (26 percent) and roots and tubers (4 percent).

such as Japan, the Republic of Korea and Thailand, because rising incomes have enabled people to eat a more varied diet.

Roots and tubers are important staples for over 1 000 million people in the developing world. They account for roughly 40 percent of the food eaten by half the population of sub-Saharan Africa. They are high in carbohydrates, calcium and vitamin C, but low in protein.

Per caput consumption of roots and tubers has been falling in many countries since the beginning of the 1970s, mainly because urban populations have found it cheaper and easier to buy imported cereals. Since 1970, consumption of roots and tubers in the Pacific Islands has fallen by 8 percent, while cereal consumption jumped by 40 percent, from 61 to 85 kilograms per person.

Many countries are experiencing a similar shift away from traditional foods, but there is growing recognition of the importance of traditional food crops in nutrition. After years of being considered "poor people's foods" some of these crops are now enjoying a comeback. Cassava, considered a minor crop at the turn of the century, has now become one of the developing world's most important staples providing a basic diet for around 500 million people. Plantings are increasing faster than for any other crop. Quinoa, a grain grown in the high Andes, is also gaining wider acceptance even outside of Latin America with the introduction of new varieties and improved processing.

Proportions of food in average diets

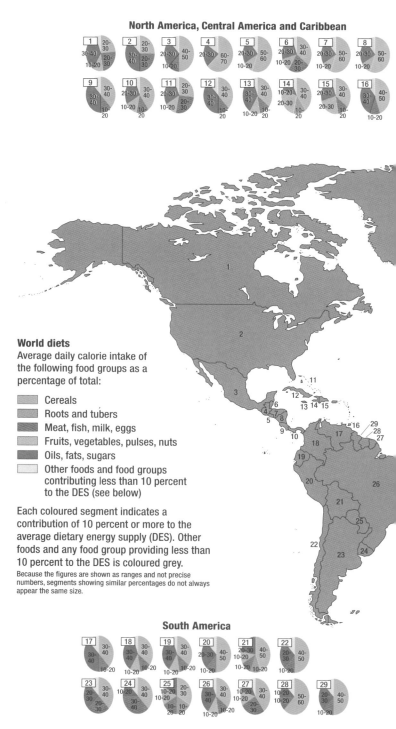

North America, Central America and Caribbean

World diets
Average daily calorie intake of the following food groups as a percentage of total:

- Cereals
- Roots and tubers
- Meat, fish, milk, eggs
- Fruits, vegetables, pulses, nuts
- Oils, fats, sugars
- Other foods and food groups contributing less than 10 percent to the DES (see below)

Each coloured segment indicates a contribution of 10 percent or more to the average dietary energy supply (DES). Other foods and any food group providing less than 10 percent to the DES is coloured grey.

Because the figures are shown as ranges and not precise numbers, segments showing similar percentages do not always appear the same size.

South America

Boundaries of newly formed nations (in former USSR, in former Yugoslavia, in former Czechoslovakia, Eritrea) are shown in grey. Data for these countries not available.

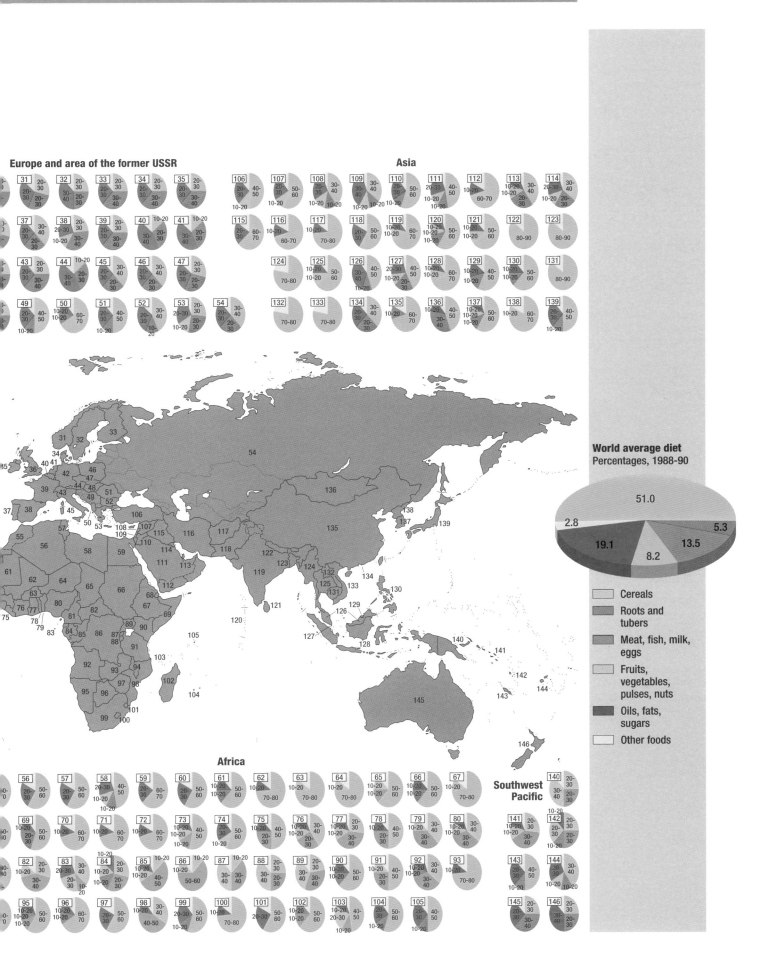

Europe and area of the former USSR

Asia

Africa

Southwest Pacific

World average diet
Percentages, 1988-90

51.0
2.8
5.3
19.1
8.2
13.5

☐ Cereals
▨ Roots and tubers
▨ Meat, fish, milk, eggs
☐ Fruits, vegetables, pulses, nuts
▨ Oils, fats, sugars
☐ Other foods

THE WORLD'S FORGOTTEN FOODS

Some traditional food plants could become foods of the future – a convenient source of income, improved nutrition and increased food supply.

Amaranth and quinoa – grains that originally came from the Andes and were holy to the Incas of Peru and the Aztecs of Mexico – are being re-evaluated. Both are versatile and nutritious. They are also hardy: amaranth thrives in hot climates; quinoa is frost resistant and can be grown as high as 4 000 metres.

Many more traditional foods await development and wider use.

Other important nutritional sources – complementary foods

Throughout the world, complementary foods play an essential role in meeting nutrient requirements. They include protein sources – meat, poultry, fish, legumes and milk products; energy sources – fats, oils and sugars; and vitamin and mineral sources – fruits, vegetables and animal products.

In addition to conventional crops and agricultural products, the following are valuable sources of nutrition. Their importance is particularly obvious during seasonal and emergency shortages.

Wild animals including insects, birds, fish, rodents and larger mammals are often the only source of animal protein for rural people. In parts of the Peruvian Amazon, for example, over 85 percent of dietary animal protein is from the wild. Some 62 developing countries rely on wildlife for at least one-fifth of their animal protein.

Tree foods and home gardens contribute significantly to rural diets. In West Java, Indonesia, coconut trees and home gardens produce 32 percent of total dietary protein and 44 percent of total calorie needs. In Puerto Rico, the produce from home gardens has increased vitamin A and C intake, especially in children.

Wild plants are essential for many rural subsistence households; at least 1 000 million people are thought to use them. In Ghana, for instance, the leaves of over 100 species of wild plants – and the fruits of another 200 – are consumed. In rural Swaziland, more than 220 species of wild plants provide a greater share of the diet than domesticated cultivars. In India, Malaysia and Thailand, about 150 wild plant species have been identified as sources of emergency food.

Fish supplements the rice diet of many north-eastern Thai and Lao farming families. Both fish and frogs are caught in streams, irrigation canals, ditches, water reservoirs and flooded paddy fields.

Forest foods can provide varied food year round, supplying essential minerals and vitamins. They include: wild leaves, seeds and nuts, fruits, roots and tubers, mushrooms, honey and animal products.

Who are the food producers?

Fruit and vegetable market, Guinea.

Population economically active in agriculture

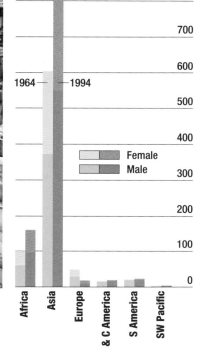

900

Millions
800

700

600

1964 —— 1994

500

400

Female
Male   300

200

100

0

Africa | Asia | Europe | N & C America | S America | SW Pacific

For every one farmer in the developed world there are 19 in the developing world. Where there is mechanization, fewer workers can produce more food.

Division of labour by gender in Africa (percentages)

0   20   40   60   80   100

Domestic work

Processing & storing crops

Weeding

Harvesting

Caring for livestock

Planting

Ploughing

☐ Women's work
▥ Men's work

O ver 1 000 million farmers work the land: men and women, young and old. Nearly all of them live in the developing world. Only a relatively small number, around 50 million, live in the developed countries where agriculture is typically highly mechanized.

Farms have been getting bigger and bigger in the developed countries as tens of thousands of small farmers, unable to make a living, have left the land. Most of North America's food is now produced by large-scale, commercial operations. Often they integrate production with food processing, marketing and distribution in a complete agribusiness system.

By contrast, farms in most of the developing world consist of small, family-owned plots, many of which have been cultivated for generations. Small farmers constitute over half the world's rural poor, but they produce about four-fifths of food supplies in developing countries.

Division of labour
The roles of men and women in food production, processing and marketing vary, but women usually play a pivotal role. In sub-Saharan Africa, they produce and market up to 90 percent of all food grown locally.

Lack of employment opportunities in rural areas gives rise to seasonal or permanent emigration, usually of men. In some parts of Africa for example, 60 percent of households are now headed by women. On average women work longer hours than men, but very few of them have title to the land they work.

Children become farm labourers at an early age, working as many as 45 hours a week in the harvest season.

Women in the developing world are almost entirely responsible for growing food for the household. And in many countries, they are also responsible for taking care of larger livestock even though the owners are usually men. In Nepal, for example, where grazing land is scarce, women are responsible for collecting fodder for the buffaloes – and a single animal can consume up to 40 tonnes of grass and leaves a year.

FARMING SYSTEMS IN THE DEVELOPING WORLD
Four broad agro-ecological zones account for 90 percent of agricultural production in developing countries. Each has a range of farming systems and a mixture of traditional and modern production systems.

Humid and per-humid lowlands
Population: 1 000 million+
Area: 3 100 million ha
Features: mostly forested areas; environmental deterioration, mainly due to loss of tree cover; reasonable food security (80 percent of root and tuber production in developing world)
Major systems: shifting cultivation; plantations (e.g. rubber); horticulture (widespread); extensive grazing (mainly in Latin America)

Hill and mountain areas
Population: 500 million+
Area: 1 000 million ha
Features: many areas with slopes of more than 30 percent gradient; most forms of environmental deterioration evident, particularly soil erosion; food insecurity increasing
Major systems: hillfarming (e.g. in Himalayas, Andes); dairy and grazing (e.g. Latin America)

Cultivators

Small-scale farmer, Peru.

An enormous range of people, from the "grain barons" of the United Kingdom's East Anglia and the United States' Midwest to the small-scale farmers of Sichuan, China, from African mothers to Indian landless labourers, till the soil for a living.

Large-scale farmers tend to specialize in one or two crops and nearly all of their produce is sold. They depend on external, often costly, inputs such as chemical fertilizer, high-yielding seeds and mechanization. The subsistence farmer, by contrast, produces as much of his family's food needs as possible and cannot usually afford expensive inputs.

Selling produce is a secondary consideration but a hoped-for bonus to make cash purchases of household essentials. Some small-scale farmers have, however, turned to producing single cash crops for income.

The merits of high input, single enterprise farming are increasingly being questioned. The need is to use inputs efficiently to keep the costs of production low while avoiding pollution and land degradation. In some instances, for example where the productive potential of the land is low or the risk of crop failure high, low input mixed farming is being encouraged. This type of farming cannot, however, produce all the tonnages needed to feed either present or future generations. Intensified mixed farming is also required.

Farming requires an array of skills: farmers must understand soil types and their limitations, know when to plant and harvest and what types of crops to rotate, when to apply organic or man-made fertilizers and pesticides, and be able to harvest and market their produce.

Poorer countries in the developing regions often lack the resources to provide much help. Where resources are available, farmers still may not receive the support that matches their needs and capabilities.

Small farmers in the developing world usually have

Forest people

Using forest products.

Nearly 500 million people live in or close to forests. Most forest peoples grow some crops but they still rely on the natural productivity of the forests.

They use many forest products: plant stems, tubers and fruits provide additional food during hungry seasons or when crops fail; wild animals are hunted for their meat and hides; and the forests provide fodder for livestock, fuelwood and medicines. Coastal mangrove forests nurture fish and crustaceans (shrimp and crabs), and provide wood for building and leaves for fodder.

Tribal people such as the Bhil, Mina and Sehariya in India depend on hill forests for wood and food, while the Maku of Colombia and Brazil, hunter-gatherers living in the upper reaches of the Amazon Basin, collect everything they need from the forest.

Pastoralists

Cattle herding, Niger.

only enough land to meet the needs of their families, or immediate community. Those able to produce surpluses for sale are at a disadvantage compared with large-scale farmers. Few small farmers have any control over the marketing and distribution of their produce, or even its price at the "farm gate". They also tend to be left out of mainstream development.

Large-scale farmers are usually able to take advantage of new harvesting techniques and other innovations. Successful farmers may buy out smallholders, who are then forced into the ranks of the landless. By 1994, there were some 500 million landless people in rural areas of developing countries – over 900 million if farmers with very little land are added in.

In order to increase food production there is a need to ensure adequate food supplies and incomes for all and to draw farmers beyond subsistence level agriculture.

Meo people, Thailand.

Pastoralists live and work in the world's drylands – ranging from the Texas rancher who runs cattle on 2 000 square kilometres of pasture to the nomadic Masai of Kenya and Tanzania who herd their cattle over their traditional rangelands. They raise livestock for their own consumption, or for sale to consumers in cities and towns, and as a source of savings. The largest meat producers, mainly in North and South America and Australia, cater for the international market, supplying North America and Asia.

Pastoralists are often better off than settled farmers during normal times. They can move their animals to follow the rains or take them to established seasonal grazing areas. They are often the first victims, however, of prolonged environmental stress – such as extended drought. Domestic animals are less able to survive until the rains return whereas crops can be stored and some,

especially new varieties, are heat tolerant and drought resistant.

Developing world pastoralists have evolved ways of making productive use of some of the world's most inhospitable areas, often moving as nomads from place to place to minimize pressure on the land.

Disaster can follow when their traditional ways are disrupted. When, for example, one African government decided to settle a nomadic population around some 200 permanent water holes, they had soon chopped down every tree in the area for use as fuelwood and building material. Their animals ate every blade of grass and every shrub, leaving a ring of desolation for kilometres around the water holes. Stripped of vegetation, the soil was soon blown away by the wind. It was found that if the nomads were allowed to return to their traditional life, the land would support twice as many people and their animals.

FARMING SYSTEMS IN THE DEVELOPING WORLD

Irrigated and naturally flooded areas
Population: 1 000 million+
Area: 215 million ha
Features: limitations include high costs, waterlogging, salinization and pollution of groundwater; crucial to food security (60 percent of grain production in developing world)
Major systems: lowland rice-based; irrigated farming (many crops); aquaculture (minor); intensive animal production; horticulture

Drylands and areas of uncertain rainfall
Population: 500 million+
Area: 3 400 million ha
Features: less than 500mm rainfall in drylands or semi-humid with light erratic rainfall; some 6 million ha lost annually through desertification; food insecurity common
Major systems: pastoral; upland cereal-based; some plantations (e.g. sisal); horticulture (on small irrigated areas)

Fisherfolk

Fishermen, Bangladesh.

Fishing fleet, Scotland.

Fish farm, China.

Artisanal fishing, Malawi.

Some 20 million fishermen ply the world's seas and inland waters or farm fish. They harvest about 100 million tonnes of fish, shellfish, invertebrates and aquatic plants every year: around 80 percent of the catch is landed by commercial operators and roughly 20 percent, largely in the developing world, by the world's 12-15 million small-scale artisanal fishermen. A further 16 million tonnes are produced by fish farmers. Over half the world's fish catch is taken by developing countries.

Fish is the world's largest wild food harvest, and provides the major source of animal protein for over 1 000 million people, most of them in Asia. It is also particularly important in the diet of such developed countries as Japan, Spain and Iceland.

In recent years, fish stocks have been seriously depleted by large-scale commercial operations on the high seas and small and medium-scale ones in waters falling under national jurisdiction. All 17 of the world's major fishing areas have either reached or exceeded their natural limits and 9 are in serious decline.

Small-scale artisanal fishermen in the tropics, who operate from canoes and small boats, are less likely to over-fish, but all too often the sheer pressure of numbers overwhelms the age-old systems for managing stocks. These traditional fishing communities are among the poorest and most neglected in the world. They often lack clean drinking water, sanitation, housing, medical care, transport and communications as well as

safe and equipped harbours and connections to markets. Outside the mainstream of economic and political life, they frequently suffer as a result of a lack of recognized rights to resources and competition from medium-scale commercial operators with better access to capital, subsidies and administrations.

The plight of these fishing communities has been increasingly recognized. For example, FAO's Bay of Bengal Programme, which was started in 1979, focuses on promoting development in small-scale fishing communities in the Bay's seven bordering countries. This, and other development programmes, operate under the assumption that if local communities receive rights and responsibilities over resources they will be better managed.

Impact of poverty on life

The poor usually live in the most undesirable areas – in deserts, in swamps, along storm-ridden coasts, on hillsides prone to landslides and avalanches, near garbage dumps or in industrial zones.

Some live on city streets in makeshift houses of cardboard or discarded wood. For much of the year they may be underemployed or completely unemployed. When they can find work it is low paid. Many survive on a diet that is inadequate for at least part of the year. They have very little money for other necessities such as education, family planning, medical care and transport.

The following profiles from different parts of the world are typical of the daily lives of poor families.

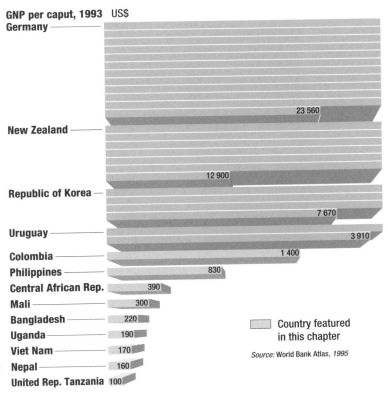

GNP per caput, 1993 US$

Country	US$
Germany	
	23 560
New Zealand	
	12 900
Republic of Korea	
	7 670
Uruguay	3 910
Colombia	1 400
Philippines	830
Central African Rep.	390
Mali	300
Bangladesh	220
Uganda	190
Viet Nam	170
Nepal	160
United Rep. Tanzania	100

☐ Country featured in this chapter

Source: World Bank Atlas, *1995*

Poor people need to be resourceful because they often live in hostile physical environments completely lacking amenities.

Rural family: Bangladesh

A typical poor farm family in Bangladesh has six members and lives in a dilapidated thatched house with earth floors. Their water comes from a well shared with about 150 other people. There is no sewage disposal; families share pit latrines, or use the waterways.

The family grows two rice crops a year on a tiny 0.1 hectare plot, but the meagre harvest meets only about one-fifth of the family's food needs. Members of the family must work on neighbouring farms to earn money to buy the rest. Nearly 90 percent of the family's spending is on food; what little remains is used for clothing,

medicines and schooling. With the passage of time their wages have bought less and less rice.

On average, the family members eat approximately 1 700 calories each per day. As a result they are well below normal weight and height. Two children had died before reaching their second birthdays.

In times of crisis such as famine or flood, the family would first sell household possessions, then tools and finally their land. It would then join the growing number of the landless.

Those families who can hold on to their land do not necessarily fare better; they often fall deep in debt to money lenders – a treadmill from which it is very hard to escape.

Industrial labourer's family: Colombia

This urban family of six lives in a shared, rented house in a shanty town on the edge of Bogota. The house has electricity and running water, but no sanitation.

The father's work, manual labour on construction sites, is heavy. The mother takes care of three school-age children and a baby, as well as doing domestic work. Their total income rarely exceeds the minimum wage: 20 percent of it is spent on rent, 70 percent on food, and the rest on transport, education, health services and recreation.

The family gets 29 percent of its dietary energy from cereals (rice, wheat and maize), 18 percent from sugar and 10 percent from potatoes and cassava. The family eats 8 400 calories of food a day, unequally shared, with the father eating most because of his heavy work.

The children are all short for their age and under-weight because they do not eat enough food. And they suffer from diarrhoea, respiratory infections and parasites.

The minimum wage has kept only slightly ahead of the cost of living, but food prices have risen faster than inflation as a whole.

The father is frequently unemployed because work in the building industry is irregular. When the father is out of work the rent still has to be paid and the family has to buy food on credit at a high-priced local store.

Small-scale fishing family: Tanzania

The fisherman's family lives on Kerebe Island, on Lake Victoria. There are six children. Small-scale farmers and landless farm labourers and their families migrate to the island in the fishing season, which lasts from May until the rains come in September. The men fish, while the women earn money by processing the catch.

The family lives in a flimsy grass house and shares a pit latrine. There is no electricity or running water.

Bananas are the major food grown on the island and families often raise goats and poultry. Most of the island's staple foods – maize, cassava flour, rice and beans – must be brought in from the mainland. The fisherman eats

two meals a day of a simple bean and banana porridge flavoured with fish sauce made from a small sardine called *dagaa* from the lake. *Dagaa* is considered a "poor man's food" but is highly nutritious because it is eaten

whole and so supplies calcium and iron as well as other essential micronutrients.

The family's nutrition ranges from adequate to marginal, depending on income from fishing: when there is no money, they can buy no other food. Money can be borrowed and later repaid with cash or fish, but this often gets fishing families deep into debt. In normal circumstances the income is enough to buy food and some goods and to save to buy inputs for farming during the rest of the year. But frequent fishing accidents and AIDS have killed or weakened some of the most productive in the community and cut many families' incomes.

Landless family: the Philippines

This landless family of six lives in a small bamboo and palm thatch house. They have no electricity or running water and few possessions other than clothes, cooking utensils and a radio. They use kerosene for lighting and

pay a monthly fee to get drinking water from a shared tap. Their farm equipment is a sickle and a mat for drying jute.

They grow vegetables and keep a pig and a few ducks on their rented home plot. Weeding a landowner's plot gives them the right to a share of its harvest (usually one-eighth to one-sixth of the crop). This increases their security, but means that they have no income for two or three months before the harvest as there is no agricultural work at the time.

Farm work is their sole source of cash income. The entire family works at harvesting, threshing and winnowing during the two main rice harvests. In a

typical year, 65 percent of income comes from crop-share payments, 15 percent from cash wages and 20 percent from the sale of a fattened pig.

Two-thirds of the family's total spending is on food. Nearly half of their food is rice, mainly from crop-share payments, but they also eat vegetables, salt, milk, fish and, rarely, meat. The family's average dietary energy intake is 10 200 calories per day.

Their low, irregular income frequently forces them into debt: where possible they borrow from friends and neighbours to avoid the 19-25 percent monthly interest charged by money lenders. A serious illness could easily bankrupt them.

Pastoral family: Mali

A pastoral family of six lives on the parched plains of Mali in round huts built of dried stalks, which are water-resistant when new and can be erected easily. This Fulani family has a herd of 24 cattle and 10 goats and grows a crop of millet during the rainy season.

In the wet season they camp around rain ponds, which dry out by November. During the cold, dry season (November-February), the young men take most of the cattle in search of grazing. The rest of the household, with their goats, weaker animals and a few milk cows, camp on the edge of a village, and buy or barter for water.

During the hot, dry season, they move camp to a

permanent water hole.

Among the Fulani, adult men are responsible for the main herd and for most of the millet cultivation. Boys tend goats and calves. The women and girls collect fuel wood and water for domestic use, help with the harvest, pound millet and prepare meals.

The household's maximum dietary energy intake, which is in October after the harvest, is 14 700 calories per day, enough to meet their dietary needs. It is at its lowest, between 7 840 and 8 820 calories per day, from December to June. The weight of both adults and children varies with the seasons.

Selling livestock accounts for over 90 percent of the

family's cash income, while half of their spending is on cereals. Prolonged drought spells disaster. In 1973, after five years of drought, 100 000 Malians perished, along with about half of their animals.

Farm family: Central African Republic

Living in a humid, subtropical climate, this family of six survives on the shifting cultivation of cassava. They live in a rudimentary hut, fashioned from mud and thatch, with no running water, electricity or sanitation. The family has no access to social services. Among such people infant mortality rates are as high as 160 per 1 000 live births and life expectancy is no more than 40 years.

Once the soil becomes unproductive after a few years of cultivation, the family moves on to clear another part of the forest. Sometimes, larger, community-level moves are organized by the village elders. The family shares the workload; it cannot count on any external help.

The family grows bananas, yams and some vegetables, which partly cover their vitamin needs. It owns no livestock other than a few chickens and perhaps a goat or two. Most of its meat comes from hunting and fishing. The average food consumption is around 2 000 calories per person per day.

Overall, the total availability of calories is adequate, but the family is continuously at risk of severe malnutrition because it depends heavily on cassava, lacks animal protein and its members suffer frequent attacks of debilitating diseases.

Farm family: Nepal

A typical hill farmer in Nepal has a family of six and lives in a small hamlet of about 30 households on terraced slopes in the lower hills of the Himalayas. The family home is made from mud, bricks and straw, and has dirt floors. There is no running

water or sanitation. The farmer owns his land – about half a hectare fragmented into seven or eight plots at different elevations. He owns some simple farm tools, some livestock and one draught bullock.

Most family members share the heavy workload, but the women in the community tend to work longer than the men – 11 hours as compared to 8 hours per day. Even children aged 10-14 work between 4 and 7 hours doing household chores and weeding.

The family grows maize and millet on rain-fed uplands and rice and wheat on low-lying, irrigable land. How much low-lying land a family has depends on its wealth. Crops are grown

intensively, using much labour and organic manures.

The farmer produces almost 60 percent of his family's food. He earns money to buy the rest by selling his labour, either within his village or far away in Katmandu, or even India. The family's daily food consumption amounts to around 2 100 calories per person.

Food production in Nepal's uplands has declined significantly over the past two decades. Since sons inherit equal shares of land, per caput farmland has declined; many remaining farmsteads are too small to support families of six or more individuals. Their future is bleak.

Forest family: Viet Nam

A typical family living in the Yen Lap cooperative in the remote area of Yen Houng Province, northern Viet Nam, has six members, three of whom work as labourers. Both men and women work in the rice paddies. The family also keeps pigs and buffaloes, fed and cared for by the women of the household. Its main foods are rice, cassava, cabbage and pig fat.

The production system is based on shifting cultivation, and rice productivity is low. The average yield of hill rice at only around 650 kilograms per hectare per year, is less than half that of lowland rice. Typically, the family earns only 35 percent of its household cash income from the sale of agricultural crops.

The family's food production meets just over half of their nutritional needs (58 percent). It depends on the nearby forest to provide it with the remainder. A wide selection of forest products is used, including 60 species of plants, fruits and wild animals. Five wild plant species substitute directly for rice, particularly during the three to four month "hungry" season prior to the harvest each year. Forest foods make the difference between getting by and starving.

Family suffering from AIDS: Uganda

In Uganda, where 3 million people are expected to die from HIV/AIDS between 1991 and 2010, the disease has an impact upon both infected adults and those who depend on them.

Esther, 35 years old and widowed, is the head of a household consisting of ten women and girls. She looks after her own three children and her brother's three orphaned girls, her late husband's 17-year-old daughter by another wife and her young child, and her sick stepmother.

When her brother died, Esther inherited a hectare of land on which she grows maize, groundnuts, cassava and sweet potatoes for family consumption. She does most of the work herself as the children only work on the farm on Saturdays. Sometimes she hires casual labourers to help her, and pays them in kind.

Esther also brews beer. This is very labour intensive and provides only a small profit, but she has no other way of generating the cash she needs to buy necessities such as soap, salt and fish or meat.

The family eats leftovers for breakfast and sorghum, sometimes with potatoes and greens, for dinner. During the "hungry season" in March and April, Esther works as a casual labourer for US$ 0.45 a day, enough income to provide one daily meal for her family.

Esther's own three girls are at school, but she cannot afford to continue paying the fees for the orphans, and is pessimistic about their future.

Feeding the world: The search for food security

The population of most developing countries is still growing rapidly, even though the rate of growth has slowed down. Every year the global population increases by 90 million. Most of the increase, around 95 percent, takes place in the developing world. Populations in most developed countries are increasing only slightly, if at all; in some of them, such as Germany and Hungary, they are even falling.

Taking the most conservative projections for world population growth over the next 30 years, food production will need to double in order to meet minimum requirements. Yet the land available to produce this additional food is being degraded, largely as a result of deforestation, overgrazing and poor farming practices.

FAO estimates that some 1 200 million hectares of land are affected by soil degradation. Erosion by wind and water accounts for just over 1 000 million hectares of this, with the balance caused by chemical and physical degradation.

At the same time, the availability of productive agricultural land per caput is declining in many countries because of population growth and the lack of reserves that could be brought into production.

Data from 57 developing countries show that nearly 50 percent of all farms are smaller than 1 hectare in size. Many poor farmers find that, as a result, they can no longer make a living from their land.

In the developing countries people are migrating in large numbers to towns and cities in search of paid employment and better opportunities. Nearly 70 percent of all Latin Americans now live in urban areas compared to just 30 percent or so 30 years ago. Urban areas are growing by 6-8 percent a year in sub-Saharan Africa. Soon, more people will live in towns and cities than in the countryside in developing countries as a whole. The young and more vigorous people tend to migrate, leaving women, children and the old to carry the burden of work.

Food services have grown up to provide for city workers and others who spend most of the day far from home. Street vendors, restaurants, fast food chains and caterers are important in almost every country. In Malaysia, for example, street food sales from the 100 000 or more vendors are estimated to have an annual value of more than US$ 2 000 million.

In the developing world, street vendors usually sell traditional dishes that are produced locally. They provide

Urban and rural population projections in developing countries
Millions (and percentage of population)

Rural 2 519 (68.8)

Urban 1 144 (31.2)

1985

Rural 3 046 (53.8)

Urban 2 612 (46.2)

2010

Growth rates, 1985-2010 (percent)

Rural: 0.8

Urban: 3.4

Total: 1.8

Ingredients for food security

WATER & SANITATION · POLITICAL STRUCTURES · LAND & WATER · ADVERTISING · FARM EQUIPMENT & INPUTS · EXCHANGE RATES · KITCHEN FUEL · HEALTH CARE · STORAGE FACILITIES · RADIO, TV & NEWSPAPERS · GOVER... · RESEARCH & DEVELO... · EMPLOYMEN... · INCOME · DISTRIBUTION · RESOURCE MANAGEMENT · FAMILY & CULTURE · PREPARED FOOD PROCESSING · MONEY & CREDIT · EDUCATION · TRANSPORT

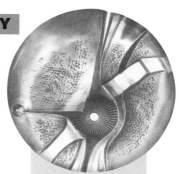

...verty is the root cause of food ...ecurity. A food secure country ...n produce, store or import the ...od it needs and distribute it ...uitably. Food insecure countries ...ically have either large numbers ...very poor people, or very low ...erage food consumption levels, ...large fluctuations in food ...pplies coupled with low ...nsumption levels.

...No single recipe will ensure ...d security for all individuals, ...useholds or nations. The basic ...gredients, illustrated here, are ...ll-known, although their quality ...d availability vary greatly from ...gion to region.

...Making people's nutritional well-...ing the focus of national and ...ernational development policies ...nd using it as a measure of ...eir success – would be a major ...p in creating a well-fed world.

Agriculture and population

Growth of world population
Thousand millions, 1950-2100

Source: UNFPA

Year	Developed	Developing
2100	1.3	10.0
2025	1.3	7.2
2010	1.3	5.9
2000	1.3	5.0
1990	1.2	4.1
1980	1.1	3.4
1970	1.0	2.7
1960	0.9	2.1
1950	0.8	1.7

Developed countries

Developing countries

World agricultural production and population   Index, 1961=100

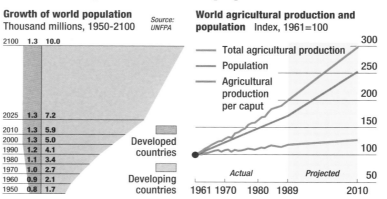

— Total agricultural production
— Population
— Agricultural production per caput

Actual *Projected*

1961 1970 1980 1989 2010

The world's ten largest urban agglomerations by the year 2000   Millions

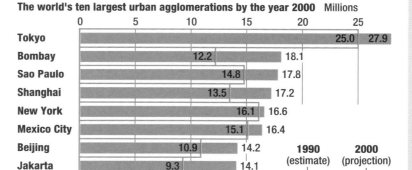

City	1990 (estimate)	2000 (projection)
Tokyo	25.0	27.9
Bombay	12.2	18.1
Sao Paulo	14.8	17.8
Shanghai	13.5	17.2
New York	16.1	16.6
Mexico City	15.1	16.4
Beijing	10.9	14.2
Jakarta	9.3	14.1
Lagos	7.7	13.5
Los Angeles	11.5	13.1

To feed the world population in the year 2025, predicted to be 8 500 million, current world food production will have to more than double.

What is food security?

Food security exists when "all people at all times have access to the food they need for a healthy active life".

Achieving food security depends on four key factors:

Availability of adequate food supplies – there must be enough food to ensure that each person's daily energy and nutrient needs can be met.

Access to sufficient food – even in a country with adequate food supplies, food security does not exist for those who cannot afford to buy enough and/or grow their own.

Stability of supplies – severe fluctuations in food availability or accessibility, caused by such factors as droughts, floods, sharp price increases or seasonal unemployment, leave people vulnerable.

Cultural acceptability – use of certain foods, food combinations or handling methods can be preempted by religious or cultural taboos.

a ready market for farmers and home gardeners. Many poor families also depend on them. For those living in shanty towns, they may be the only source of cooked food.

Many street vendors offer good nutritious food, but some sell products of questionable hygiene and safety. As a result, where street foods are widespread vendors need to be trained and standards introduced to ensure good hygiene and provide food free from harmful contamination.

About one-third of the people in cities of the developing world live in desperately overcrowded slums and squatter settlements.

Pressures on resources for food production

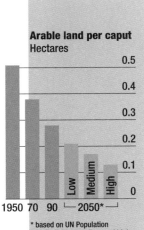

Arable land per caput
Hectares

0.5
0.4
0.3
0.2
0.1
0

Low   Medium   High

1950 70 90 └─ 2050* ─┘

* based on UN Population
Division's low, medium and high
population projections

Although the volume of agricultural production has doubled over the past 30 years, this progress has bypassed many countries and peoples: in sub-Saharan Africa nutritional levels have actually fallen since the 1970s.

Poverty is the root cause of undernutrition in a world which has been able to increase overall food production. The major problem is that the increases are spread unevenly around the globe, and that the poor cannot afford to buy what is produced.

An increasing population has to live off a dwindling supply of arable land and increasingly limited water resources. There is a vicious circle between increasing poverty and resource degradation. This makes it vital to achieve sustainable forms of agriculture.

Sustainable agricultural and rural development conserves land, water and plant and animal genetic resources. It is environmentally non-degrading and technically appropriate, as well as being economically viable and socially acceptable.

Some improvements are already accessible to the small farmers who form the majority of food producers. They include a range of farming practices designed to reduce the need for high levels of expensive farm inputs such as chemical fertilizers and pesticides. Integrated plant nutrition uses a combination of organic and mineral sources of soil nutrients with tillage and crop rotation to increase crop production; and integrated pest management (IPM) which reduces the need for chemical pesticides by making use of biological controls to minimize disease and damage by pests.

To achieve sustainable food production and security, poor farmers need access to finance and productive resources, including advice and technical help. Rural incomes, status of women, diets and food distribution systems need to be improved. Agricultural waste will have to be reduced. Land and other resources will have to be distributed more equitably. At the same time, progress in reducing population growth will help relieve pressure on resources and bring food production and supplies into balance with needs and demand.

International Conference on Nutrition

In December 1992, some 159 countries and the European Community gathered in Rome for the International Conference on Nutrition. Organized jointly by FAO and WHO, the Conference adopted a broad-based plan of action to combat malnutrition.

The Conference had nine major themes:

● Improving household food security

● Preventing and managing infectious diseases

● Promoting breast-feeding

● Caring for the socio-economically deprived and nutritionally vulnerable

● Promoting appropriate diets and healthy lifestyles

● Protecting consumers through improved food quality and safety

● Preventing and combating specific micronutrient deficiencies

● Assessing, analysing and monitoring nutrition levels

● Incorporating nutrition objectives into development policies and programmes.

The participating states agreed to take all necessary steps to eliminate, before the end of this decade:

● Famine and famine-related deaths

● Starvation and nutritional deficiency diseases in communities affected by natural and man-made disasters

● Iodine and vitamin A deficiencies.

They also pledged to reduce substantially within this decade:

● Starvation and widespread chronic hunger

● Undernutrition, especially among children, women and the aged

● Other important micronutrient deficiencies, including iron

● Diet-related communicable and non-communicable diseases

● Social and other impediments to optimal breast-feeding

● Inadequate sanitation and poor hygiene, including unsafe drinking water.

By 1995, some 90 countries were launching national programmes designed to reduce malnutrition and improve diets.

REPUBLIQUE DE GUINEE

Conférence Internationale sur
la Nutrition

150F

Protect and Produce

Dimensions of Need

The soil

Fertile soil ready for planting chick peas, Jordan.

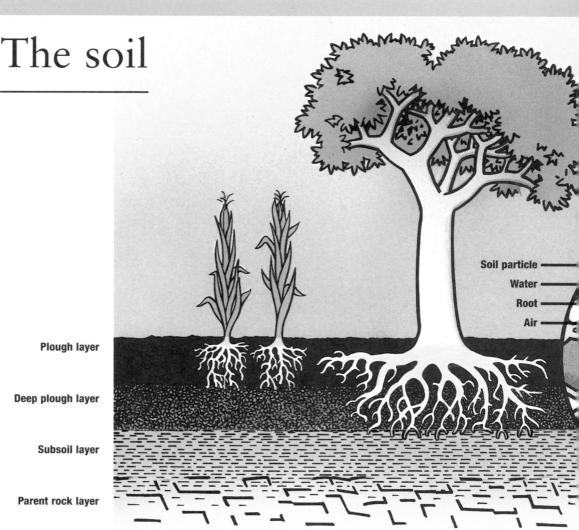

Plough layer

Deep plough layer

Subsoil layer

Parent rock layer

Soil particle

Water

Root

Air

Soil limits agriculture
Percentages of total world land area

23

22

28

10

6

11

☐ Soil too dry
☐ Chemical problems
☐ Soil too shallow
▨ Soil too wet
☐ Permafrost
▦ No limitations

Only 11 percent of the world's soils can be farmed without being irrigated, drained or otherwise improved.

Soil covers most of the land surface of the earth in a thin layer, ranging in thickness from a few centimetres to several metres. It is composed of inorganic matter (rock and mineral particles), organic matter (decaying plants and animals), living plants and animals (many of them microscopic), water and air.

Basically, soil forms as rocks slowly crumble away. Air and water collect between the particles, and chemical changes occur. Plants take root, binding the particles together, shielding the surface from the elements, drawing up minerals from lower layers and attracting animal life. Bacteria and fungi break down plant and animal remains into fertile humus.

The speed of this process varies. In prairie regions with ample rain and organic inputs, it may take 50 years to build up a few centimetres of soil; in mountainous areas it can take thousands of years. The process of destruction as a result of misuse or erosion is much quicker. Once completely destroyed, soil is for all practical purposes lost for ever.

Fertile soils teem with life. Porous loamy soils are the richest of all, laced with organic matter which retains water and provides the nutrients needed by crops. Sand and clay soils tend to have less organic matter and have drainage problems: sand is very porous and clay is impermeable. Only 11 percent of the earth's soils have no inherent limitations for agriculture. The rest are either too wet, too dry, too shallow, chemically unsuitable or permanently frozen.

To grow, plants need nitrogen, phosphorus, potassium and a range of other elements. However fertile the soil, growing crops will use up its nutrients. Farmers once compensated for this by spreading animal manure and plant waste on their fields. Increasingly, these have been replaced by man-made fertilizers.

Organic matter maintains the soil structure. It also acts as a buffer for chemical fertilizers, adding to their beneficial effects and reducing possible harm. In fact, the organic content and structure of the soil has to be managed as carefully as the nutrient content.

As agriculture has become more intensive and extensive, mineral fertilizer use has increased. Between 1981 and 1991, the world's annual use of fertilizers rose from 81 to 96 kilograms per hectare of

A profile of the soil reveals a sequence of horizons, varying in colour and texture according to their composition. Plant roots work their way between the soil particles, binding and aerating the soil.

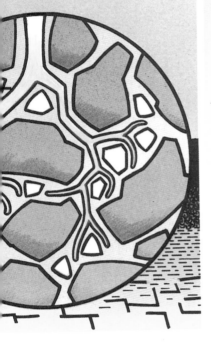

Soil texture variation

Percent clay

Percent silt

Clay

Silty clay

Sandy clay

Clay loam

Silty clay loam

Sandy clay loam

Loam

Sandy loam

Silty loam

Loamy sand

Sand

Silt

Percent sand

Source: Geography in Diagrams, *CUP*

Soil texture varies with particle size from clay (fine) through silt (medium) to sand (coarse). The larger the particles the larger the spaces between them so water drains fast through sand but clay gets waterlogged quickly. Texture depends largely on the bedrock – shales yield finer soils than sandstones – but most soils contain a mixture of particle sizes in different proportions. Loam is best for plant growth.

Soil fertility is a key factor in determining agricultural potential. All plants take up nutrients from the soil as they grow; these nutrients are removed with any plant that is harvested. Crop rotation or fertilizers are required to prevent even the best soils being depleted by farming.

cropland. This average, however, conceals huge differences in usage – Zimbabwe, one of Africa's higher users, used only 56 kilograms per hectare a year in 1989-91.

When fertilizer levels correspond to the needs of specific soils and crops and the structure of soil is conserved, yields can be sustained indefinitely. Over-use or under-use of fertilizer can lead to crop failures. Over-application can also cause pollution: excess nutrients leach out of the soil into groundwater, streams, rivers and lakes, making their water unfit for consumption or boosting the growth of algae, which can suffocate entire aquatic ecosystems.

The production of food depends on healthy agricultural systems. These in turn depend on healthy soils.

Fertilizer use

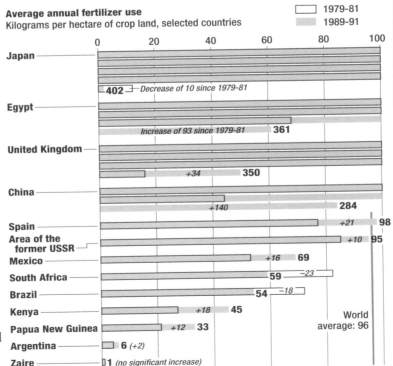

Average annual fertilizer use
Kilograms per hectare of crop land, selected countries

☐ 1979-81
▧ 1989-91

Japan	**402** Decrease of 10 since 1979-81	
Egypt	Increase of 93 since 1979-81 **361**	
United Kingdom	+34 **350**	
China	+140 **284**	
Spain	+21 **98**	
Area of the former USSR	+10 **95**	
Mexico	+16 **69**	
South Africa	**59** −23	
Brazil	**54** −18	
Kenya	+18 **45**	
Papua New Guinea	+12 **33**	
Argentina	**6** (+2)	
Zaire	**1** (no significant increase)	

World average: 96

Maize farming experiment, Nicaragua. Scientists will use the results to teach local farmers how best to cultivate and fertilize their land. In the absence of any constraints such as availability of water, judicious use of fertilizers can raise yields by 30 percent, but over-use can do more harm than good.

TYPICAL SOIL PROFILES

Luvisols present few problems for agriculture. With moderate management they can be extremely productive.

Gleysols are poorly drained. With appropriate drainage and water control, however, they can be developed to at least medium agricultural potential.

Vertisols are dark clays and difficult to work. Good management can bring them to medium or high potential.

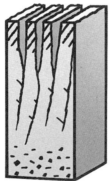

Ferralsols are acid and found in tropical or subtropical lowlands. With appropriate management they offer medium to high potential for selected crops.

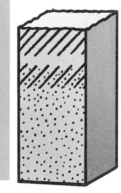

Soils either too dry or too cold
Shallow soils
Sandy soils
Dark clays
Saline soils
Acid soils of tropical/subtropical lowlands
Soils of tropical/subtropical highlands
Ferruginous soils
Poorly drained soils
Soils with few problems

KEY

~~ Open surface	Stable mineral matter	Salinity
— Sealed surface	Unstable mineral matter	Sodicity
Organic matter	Slow permeability	Rock

Main soil association	Soils too dry	Soils too cold	Shallow soils	Sandy
Soil components	Hot deserts: Calcisols, Gypsisols and shifting sand dunes	Very cold areas: Permafrost, gelic soil units, glaciers	Leptosols and lithic phases of other soils. Rocky terrain	Arenos Regos Podzo soils v coarse
Agricultural potential	Nil for rain-fed agriculture; medium to high locally when irrigation is possible	Nil or very low	Generally low. Some potential for grazing	Low t depen nutrie moistu mana level

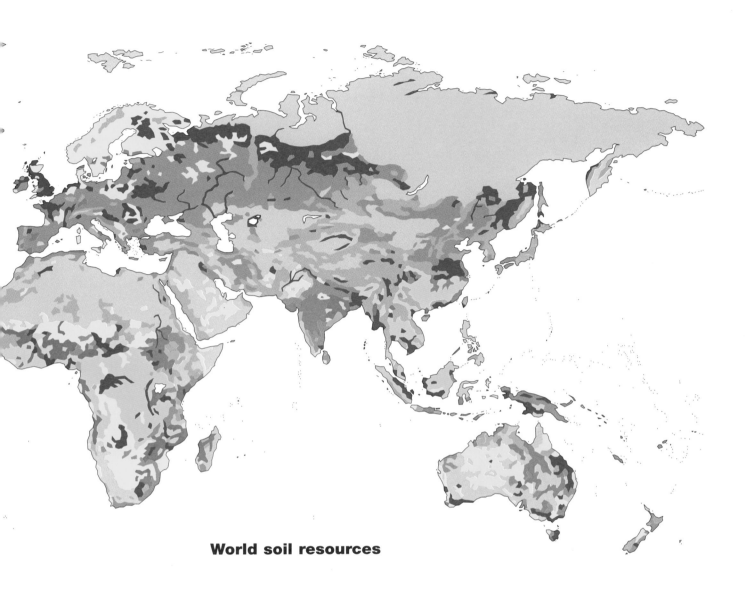

World soil resources

k clays	Saline soils	Acid soils of sub/tropical lowlands	Soils of sub/tropical highlands	Ferruginous (iron-rich) soils	Poorly drained soils	Soils with few problems
isols, vertic units	Solonchaks, Solonetz, saline and sodic phases of other soil units. Salt flats	Ferralsols, Acrisols, Alisols, dystric and humic Nitisols, Petroferric phases of other soils	Andosols, euric Nitisols	Ferric Luvisols, Lixisols, ferralic Cambisols	Gleysols, Fluvisols, Histosols, Planosols, gleyic soil units	Luvisols, Cambisols, Chernozems, Kastanozems, Phaeozems; Podzoluvisols, Greyzems
kability problems, medium to high en well managed	Generally low. Reclaimed land has low to medium production potential	Medium to high (Nitisols) with adapted crop selection and management	Medium to high if phosphorus fixation problems are overcome	Only medium potential, even with good management	Medium to high potential with adapted water and drainage control. Low in Histosols, Planosols and acid sulphate Fluvisols	High to very high with moderate to good management; low (but with forestry potential) for Podzoluvisols, Greyzems

Water: A finite resource

Although water covers 75 percent of the world's surface, 97.5 percent of the earth's water is salt water; of the remaining 2.5 percent, most is locked away as groundwater or in glaciers.

Without water our planet would be a barren wasteland. Of the three main ways in which people use water – municipal (drinking water and sewage treatment), industrial and agricultural (mostly irrigation) – farming accounts for the largest part, some 65 percent globally in 1990.

Water is a finite resource: there are some 1 400 million cubic kilometres on earth and circulating through the hydrological cycle. Nearly all of this is salt water and most of the rest is frozen or under ground. Only one-hundredth of 1 percent of the world's water is readily available for human use.

This would be enough to meet humanity's needs – if it were evenly distributed. But it is not. In Malaysia 100 people share each million cubic metres of water; in India, the figure is 350 and in Israel, 4 000. And where there is water, it is often polluted: nearly a third of the population of developing countries has no access to safe drinking water.

In many countries, the amount of water available to each person is falling, as populations rise. By the year 2000, Latin America's per caput water resources will have fallen by nearly three-quarters since 1950. In the twenty-first century the main constraint on development in Egypt will be access to water, not land. Over 230 million people live in countries – most of them in Africa or the Near East – where less than 1 000 cubic metres of water is available per person each year.

Even countries with greater supplies are extracting too much from their underground water reserves. The water table under Beijing is sinking by 2 metres every year, while Bangkok's has fallen by 25 metres since the 1950s. The level of the vast Ogallala aquifer, which lies beneath eight US states, is dropping by nearly 1 metre a year.

Pollution exacerbates the problem. Some 450 cubic kilometres of waste water are poured into the world's surface waters every year: two-thirds of the world's available runoff is used to dilute and bear it away.

A world short of water is also an unstable world. More than 200 river systems cross international boundaries, and 13 rivers and lakes are shared by 96 countries. Over-use or pollution by countries upstream can be devastating for those downstream. Access to water, particularly in areas where rainfall is low or erratic, is becoming a major political issue and vital to national interests.

Faced with these crises, the world must learn to be less wasteful and to manage its water resources better. Methods include conserving supplies, using reservoirs and small dams to catch runoff, recharging aquifers, protecting watersheds and recycling waste water in agriculture and industry.

Where the water is

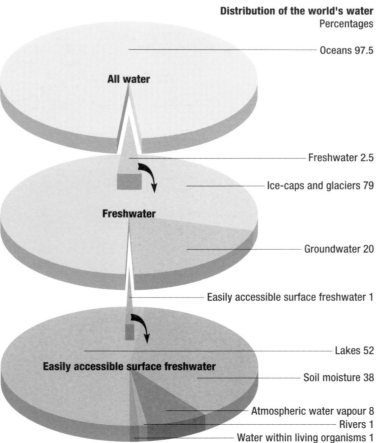

Distribution of the world's water
Percentages

All water

Oceans 97.5

Freshwater 2.5

Ice-caps and glaciers 79

Freshwater

Groundwater 20

Easily accessible surface freshwater 1

Lakes 52

Easily accessible surface freshwater

Soil moisture 38

Atmospheric water vapour 8

Rivers 1

Water within living organisms 1

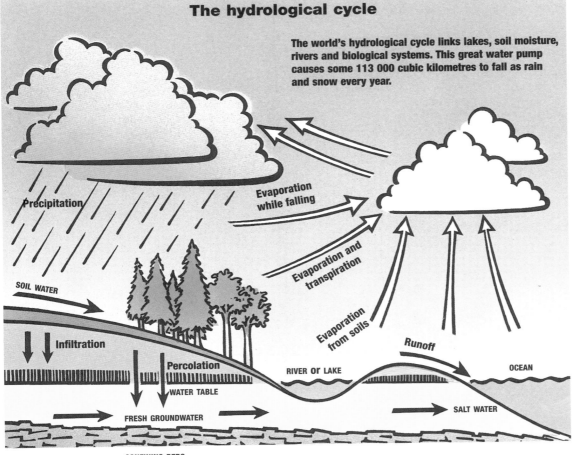

The hydrological cycle

The world's hydrological cycle links lakes, soil moisture, rivers and biological systems. This great water pump causes some 113 000 cubic kilometres to fall as rain and snow every year.

Precipitation

Evaporation while falling

Evaporation and transpiration

SOIL WATER

Evaporation from soils

Runoff

Infiltration

Percolation

RIVER or LAKE

OCEAN

WATER TABLE

FRESH GROUNDWATER

SALT WATER

CONFINING BEDS

All life depends on water. Although overall the world's population can count on a supply of about 9 000 cubic kilometres of freshwater per year, it is not evenly distributed. Hydrologists regard countries where indigenous water supplies average less than 1 000 cubic metres per person per year as "water-scarce".

Water availability and water scarcity

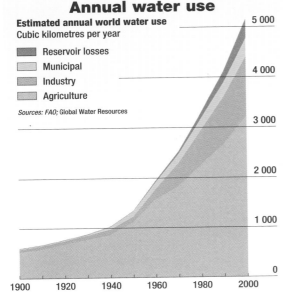

Annual water use

Estimated annual world water use
Cubic kilometres per year

- Reservoir losses
- Municipal
- Industry
- Agriculture

Sources: FAO; Global Water Resources

5 000
4 000
3 000
2 000
1 000
0

1900   1920   1940   1960   1980   2000

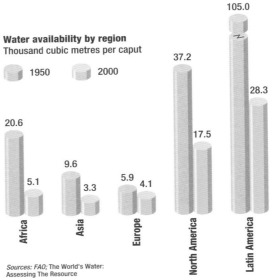

Water availability by region
Thousand cubic metres per caput

1950   2000

Africa — 20.6 / 5.1
Asia — 9.6 / 3.3
Europe — 5.9 / 4.1
North America — 37.2 / 17.5
Latin America — 105.0 / 28.3

Sources: FAO; The World's Water: Assessing The Resource

Water-scarce countries
(based on less than 1 000 cubic metres available per caput per year)

Since 1955
Bahrain, Barbados, Djibouti, Jordan, Kuwait, Malta, Singapore

Since 1990
Algeria, Burundi, Cape Verde, Israel, Kenya, Malawi, Qatar, Rwanda, Saudi Arabia, Somalia, Tunisia, United Arab Emirates, Yemen

By 2025*
Comoros, Egypt, Ethiopia, Haiti, Iran, Libya, Morocco, Oman, South Africa, Syria
**Peru, Tanzania, Zimbabwe
***Cyprus

*   on UN population projections
**   on medium projections
*** on high projection only

Finding enough water can be a formidable task. Water-scarce countries must balance strategies for increasing water supply against risks of upsetting the delicate balance of the local ecosystem.

Irrigation losses
Percentages

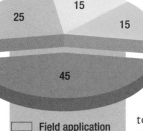

- ⬜ Field application losses
- ⬜ Farm distribution losses
- ⬜ Transmission to farm
- ⬛ **Water effectively used by crop**

Irrigation

Irrigation systems have existed for almost as long as settled agriculture. Five thousand years ago, the ancient Egyptians used the waters of the Nile to irrigate their crops. Two thousand years later, the great civilizations of the Fertile Crescent, stretching from the eastern Mediterranean to the Persian Gulf, were built on irrigated agriculture.

Irrigation is essential to feeding the world. Although only 17 percent of the world's cropland is irrigated, it produces over 33 percent of our food, making it roughly two and a half times as productive as rain-fed agriculture.

In spite of the pressing need for expansion, less new land is now being brought under irrigation than in the early 1970s. This is because of the shortage of suitable land, the rising cost of constructing irrigation systems and the scarcity of water itself.

Bureaucratic interference, faulty management, lack of involvement of users, interrupted water supplies and poor construction have all led to poor performance, which has discouraged investment. In some cases up to 60 percent of the water withdrawn for use in irrigation never reaches the crops.

In addition, waterlogging and salinization have sapped the productivity of nearly 50 percent of the world's irrigated lands. Unless irrigated fields are properly drained, salts can build up in the soil, making the land infertile. Salinity affects 23 percent of China's irrigated land and 21 percent of Pakistan's.

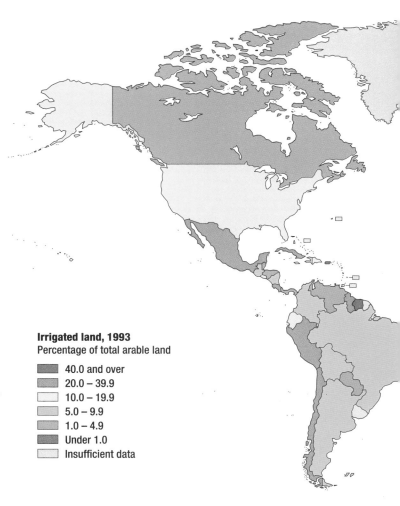

Irrigated land, 1993
Percentage of total arable land

- ⬛ 40.0 and over
- ⬛ 20.0 – 39.9
- ⬜ 10.0 – 19.9
- ⬜ 5.0 – 9.9
- ⬛ 1.0 – 4.9
- ⬛ Under 1.0
- ⬜ Insufficient data

Overhead pivot spray (top).
Irrigation canal (middle).
Irrigational flooding (bottom).

Other problems include the accumulation of pollutants and sediments in large dams and reservoirs, and the fact that irrigation systems provide an ideal habitat for the vectors of waterborne diseases.

The key to improved irrigation lies in more efficient use of water; recycling waste water and proper drainage. Drip irrigation and low-pressure spray systems are now being used in over 20 countries to deliver water directly to crops. Small dams, located closer to agricultural areas, are replacing large ones. Canals are being lined with concrete and covered to reduce seepage and evaporation. Several countries now use treated waste water for irrigation; Israel was using up to 30 percent of its urban waste water in this way as early as 1987.

:entage of land irrigated

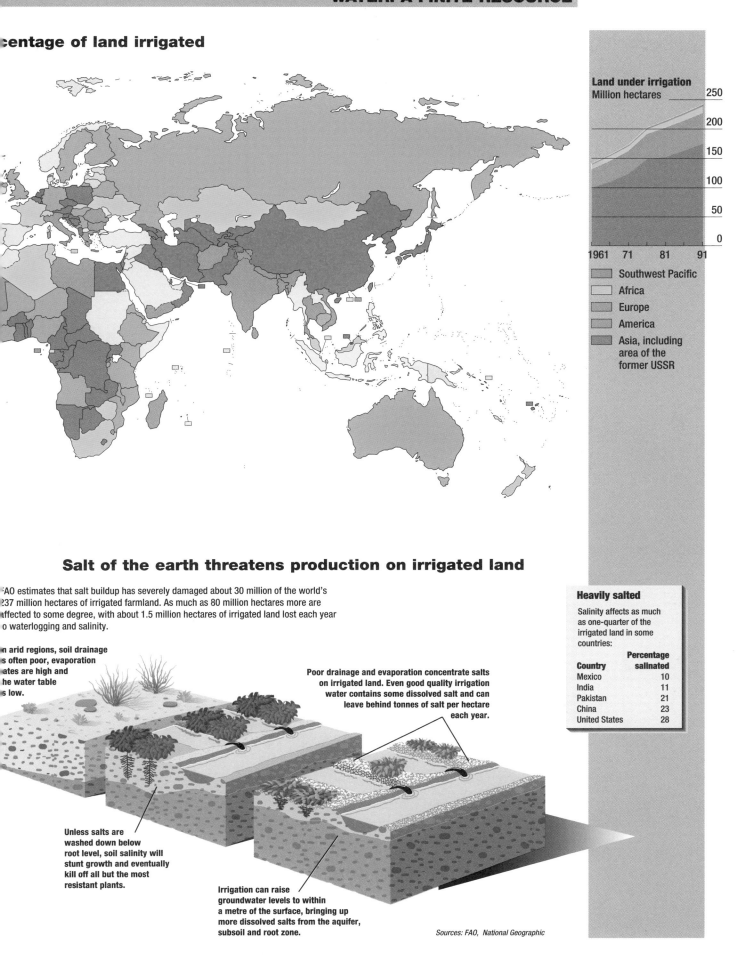

Land under irrigation
Million hectares

1961 71 81 91	250 200 150 100 50 0

- Southwest Pacific
- Africa
- Europe
- America
- Asia, including area of the former USSR

Salt of the earth threatens production on irrigated land

FAO estimates that salt buildup has severely damaged about 30 million of the world's 237 million hectares of irrigated farmland. As much as 80 million hectares more are affected to some degree, with about 1.5 million hectares of irrigated land lost each year to waterlogging and salinity.

In arid regions, soil drainage is often poor, evaporation rates are high and the water table is low.

Poor drainage and evaporation concentrate salts on irrigated land. Even good quality irrigation water contains some dissolved salt and can leave behind tonnes of salt per hectare each year.

Heavily salted

Salinity affects as much as one-quarter of the irrigated land in some countries:

Country	Percentage salinated
Mexico	10
India	11
Pakistan	21
China	23
United States	28

Unless salts are washed down below root level, soil salinity will stunt growth and eventually kill off all but the most resistant plants.

Irrigation can raise groundwater levels to within a metre of the surface, bringing up more dissolved salts from the aquifer, subsoil and root zone.

Sources: FAO, National Geographic

Restoring the land

Soil erosion by water, Costa Rica. It is estimated that, worldwide, 5-7 million hectares of land valuable to agriculture are lost every year through erosion and degradation.

Soil erosion is a natural phenomenon: it has occurred over the millenia as part of geological processes and climate change. However, erosion is more severe now: globally, moderate to severe soil degradation affects almost 2 000 million hectares of arable and grazing land – an area larger than that of the United States and Mexico combined. More than 55 percent of this damage is caused by water erosion and nearly 33 percent by wind erosion.

Every year soil erosion and other forms of land degradation rob the world of 5-7 million hectares of farming land. Every year 25 000 million tonnes of topsoil are washed away: China's Huang River alone dumps 1 600 million tonnes a year into the sea. The United States has lost about one-third of its topsoil since settled agriculture began. Worldwide, soil erosion puts the livelihoods of nearly 1 000 million people at risk.

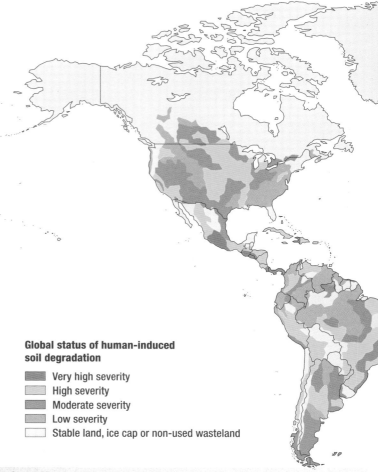

Global status of human-induced soil degradation

- Very high severity
- High severity
- Moderate severity
- Low severity
- Stable land, ice cap or non-used wasteland

Impact of soil erosion

1 Deforestation
2 Steep land being cultivated down the slope
3 Monocrops grown over large areas
4 Landslide blocks road
5 Fish catch reduced in shallow waters
6 Siltation cuts hydroelectric plant's lifespan
7 Gully erosion eats into crop land
8 Mud banks reduce navigability of rivers
9 Urban slums grow as rural population migrates to the city
10 Bridge destroyed by floods
11 Crops grown on large unprotected fields
12 Wind erosion affects badly managed pasture
13 Frequently flooded village is deserted

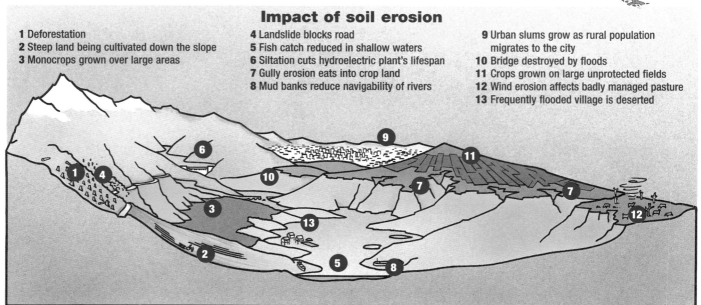

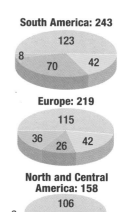

Degraded soils

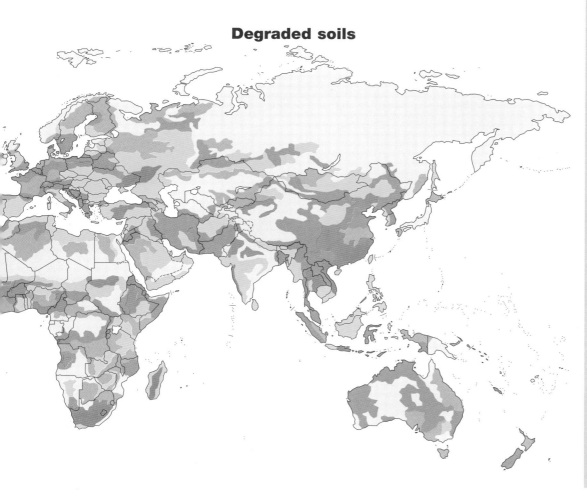

Overgrazing and deforestation leave the land prone to erosion. Vegetation renewal can reduce further damage, binding the soil and protecting it from the destructive action of wind and rain.

Major causes of soil degradation
Percentages

34.5	Overgrazing
29.5	Deforestation
35.0	Mismanagement of arable land
1.0	Other

What are the causes of soil degradation?

Soil erosion mostly occurs when there is no vegetation to protect the soil from being washed or blown away. Clearing forests, growing crops on steep slopes or on large fields without protection, can all lead to erosion. So can ploughing too deeply, failing to rotate crops, planting crops up and down hills rather than along their contours or grazing too many animals on one piece of land. Soil degradation in developing countries is closely linked to poverty: both personal and national. Poor farmers, with no resources to fall back on, may be forced to put immediate needs before the long-term health of the land. Governments, under pressure from foreign debt, weak commodity prices and the needs of their urban populations, coupled with domestic policies that are biased against agriculture, often fail to give adequate support to rural people.

Soil degradation by area and type
Million hectares

- Water erosion
- Wind erosion
- Chemical degradation
- Physical degradation

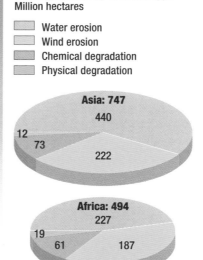

Asia: 747
440
222
73
12

Africa: 494
227
187
61
19

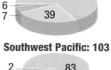

South America: 243
123
70
42
8

Europe: 219
115
42
26
36

North and Central America: 158
106
39
7
6

Southwest Pacific: 103
83
17
1
2

Fighting erosion

The effects of erosion are legion. Soil washed off bare hillsides ruins aquatic habitats and clogs waterways. Reservoirs silt up, cutting the lifespan of hydroelectric schemes. Riverbeds rise, increasing the risk of floods.

Erosion can, however, be reduced. And eroded land can be restored.

The weapons in the fight against erosion fall into two categories – biological and physical. The biological approach involves matching crops to soils, and farming methods to terrain. Physical techniques include building terraces and dams, controlling gullies (by, for instance, planting trees) and overall watershed management.

In the 1930s, wind erosion devastated millions of hectares of farmland in the United States. As a result the Government set up an agricultural extension service to train farmers in soil conservation. They were taught to farm along the contours, to plough less deeply and to plant trees, hedges and grass around the edges of fields. Crop rotation was introduced, giving soils a chance to recover nutrients, and irrigation was made available. Productivity was restored within a few years.

In 1979, the Chinese authorities, supported by the United Nations Development Programme (UNDP) and FAO, set up a project in Mizhi County on the Loess Plateau, one of the world's most eroded regions. Nearly two-thirds of the land in Mizhi slopes at an angle of over 20 degrees. Soil improvement methods included turning steep slopes over to permanent vegetation, terracing and gully control. Farmers were encouraged to replace annual crops with perennials, such as alfalfa, which would hold the soil in place from year to year, and to diversify into small animal husbandry and fruit growing. Total food production has risen by about 70 percent, in spite of the fact that the cultivated area has been halved.

In southern Morocco in the mid-1970s, palm plantations, villages and roads were being buried under wind-blown sand released by overgrazing and wood cutting. In the 1980s, three methods of stabilizing the sand dunes proved successful: using chequerboard patterns of palm branches to protect vegetation from the wind, erecting fibro-cement windbreaks and sculpting the sandbanks on road verges so as to encourage the wind to carry sand away rather than allow it to settle. These techniques saved villages, palm plantations and many irrigation canals, roads and railways from the desert.

In Niger, FAO's enormous Keita project has transformed a barren landscape into a flourishing environment for crops and livestock – so much so that the area can now be seen from space as a green patch in the desert.

Biological techniques of erosion control are the most important. Planting the right crop and growing it in the right way is much cheaper than physical protection and can give immediate returns to the farmer, encouraging wider use.

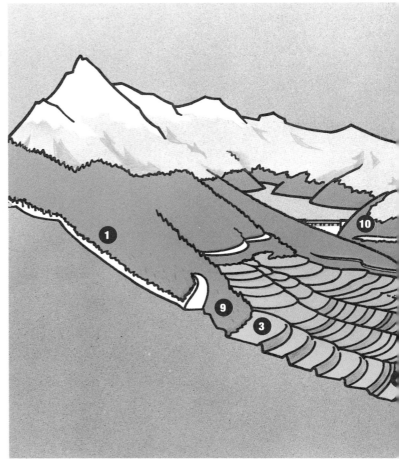

Combating soil erosion

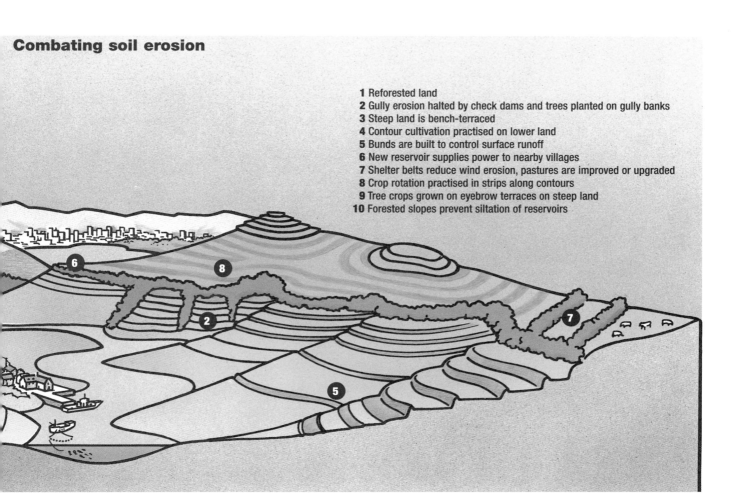

1 Reforested land
2 Gully erosion halted by check dams and trees planted on gully banks
3 Steep land is bench-terraced
4 Contour cultivation practised on lower land
5 Bunds are built to control surface runoff
6 New reservoir supplies power to nearby villages
7 Shelter belts reduce wind erosion, pastures are improved or upgraded
8 Crop rotation practised in strips along contours
9 Tree crops grown on eyebrow terraces on steep land
10 Forested slopes prevent siltation of reservoirs

The Keita project in Niger. Fences built of millet stalks hinder dune migration by wind action in the long dry season (above). Check dams, built by filling wire mesh cages with stones, reduce water erosion in seasonal floods (top left). New farming techniques allow crops to be grown on land never cultivated before (left).

How many people can the land support?

Many countries are simply mining their agricultural resources and degrading, in some cases irreversibly, the very basis of their future survival and prosperity.

The earth could, in theory, feed very many more people than now inhabit the globe. But, in practice, good soils, favourable climates, rainfall and fresh water are unevenly spread around the world – and do not necessarily correspond to distribution of population. So while some countries can produce an excess of food, others struggle with inadequate resources. Many developing countries are overexploiting their soils and several need to wrest food from land poorly suited to agricultural production.

FAO has been mapping and assessing the world's land resources and agroclimates since the early 1960s. In the 1970s it began a decade-long study of 117 developing countries to see which could grow enough food on their available land for their populations. The study – carried out with the support of the United Nations Population Fund (UNFPA) and in collaboration with the International Institute for Applied Systems Analysis (IIASA) – calculated the numbers each country could theoretically support under a simplified scenario: use of all potentially arable rain-fed land (plus irrigated land) disregarding the needs for other uses, at three input levels – low (using traditional subsistence agriculture), intermediate (using some fertilizer and a combination of current and improved crop varieties) and high (the equivalent of Western European levels of farming).

It found, based on these assumptions, that even in 1975, 54 countries could not feed their populations with

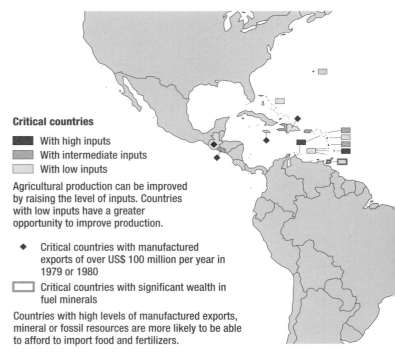

Critical countries

- ▰ With high inputs
- ▰ With intermediate inputs
- ▱ With low inputs

Agricultural production can be improved by raising the level of inputs. Countries with low inputs have a greater opportunity to improve production.

- ◆ Critical countries with manufactured exports of over US$ 100 million per year in 1979 or 1980
- ▭ Critical countries with significant wealth in fuel minerals

Countries with high levels of manufactured exports, mineral or fossil resources are more likely to be able to afford to import food and fertilizers.

Limitations on crop potential

Constraints on land with crop production potential in developing countries
Percentage of total rain-fed land area

▰ No constraints

▰ Constraints on crop production
(steep slopes, shallow soils, low natural fertility, poor soil drainage, sandy soils, stony soils, dry soils, chemical problems)

	No constraints	Constraints on crop production
Sub-Saharan Africa	28	72
North Africa and Near East	57	43
South Asia	58	42
East Asia (excluding China)	37	63
Latin America and Caribbean	28	72

traditional methods of food production and 38 percent of the entire land area – home to 1 165 million people – was carrying more inhabitants than it could theoretically support. With populations projected to the year 2000, it estimated that 64 countries – more than half the total – would be facing a critical situation; at low input levels 38 would then be unable to

support even half their projected populations. Twenty-eight of the 64 would cease to be critical if they could raise their agriculture to the intermediate level, as would another 17 if they could reach Western European standards. But 19 would still not be able to produce enough food, even then – and while some of these are wealthy enough to be able to import food, others are

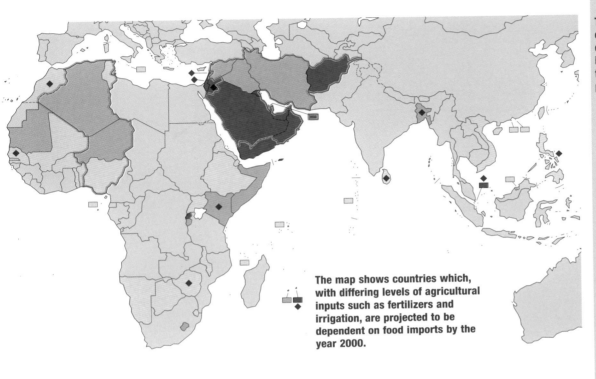

The amount of cultivable land on earth is finite, making inputs necessary to feed the increasing population.

The map shows countries which, with differing levels of agricultural inputs such as fertilizers and irrigation, are projected to be dependent on food imports by the year 2000.

Cultivated areas and gross reserves

Land under cultivation and land with crop production potential in developing countries

Million hectares

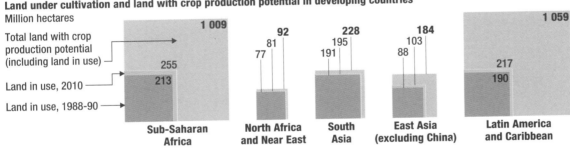

Total land with crop production potential (including land in use)

Land in use, 2010

Land in use, 1988-90

	Sub-Saharan Africa	North Africa and Near East	South Asia	East Asia (excluding China)	Latin America and Caribbean
Total land with crop production potential	1 009	92	228	184	1 059
Land in use, 2010	255	81	195	103	217
Land in use, 1988-90	213	77	191	88	190

among the poorest countries on earth.

Much of the agricultural area of a country or a region has limitations (see chart) that may make it less suitable for arable farming. 1995 FAO estimates of arable land in use compared with the area potentially suitable show similarly wide differences between regions and countries, with some

countries having essentially no arable land reserves, such as Tunisia and Burundi, and others having large amounts, for example Angola, Guyana and Brazil. Part of these gross land reserves are not available for conversion, however, because of other uses including forestry, grazing or conservation.

Against this background, FAO's 1995 study, *World*

Agriculture: Towards 2010, estimated net cereal import requirements increasing from about 8 million tonnes to 19 million tonnes for sub-Saharan Africa; 38 to 71 million tonnes for the Near East and North Africa; 27 to 35 million tonnes for East Asia (excluding China); and 5 to 10 million tonnes for South Asia, primarily as a result of shortages of arable land.

World potential land use capabilities

Much of the land in developing countries is not suited to rain-fed agriculture, but of the potentially productive land, only about one-third is cultivated. The scale of the map does not allow some important cropland areas, for example in West Africa, to be shown. Also, land shown as mainly suitable for one use may well be suited for other uses.

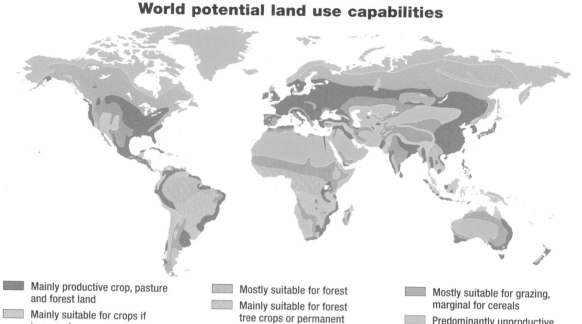

- Mainly productive crop, pasture and forest land
- Mainly suitable for crops if improved
- Mostly suitable for forest
- Mainly suitable for forest tree crops or permanent pastures
- Mostly suitable for grazing, marginal for cereals
- Predominantly unproductive land

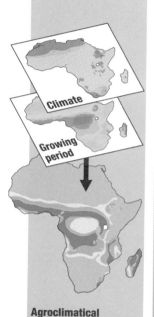

Agroclimatical information, when combined with soil data, indicates where crops can best be grown.

Five steps to getting the best use from the land

To help identify the optimum sustainable use for all cultivable land in the developing world, an FAO study demonstrated which land, down to 10 square kilometres, is best suited to each of the 11 major crops grown in the developing world. These data are of vital importance to developing world governments striving to provide food security for their populations.

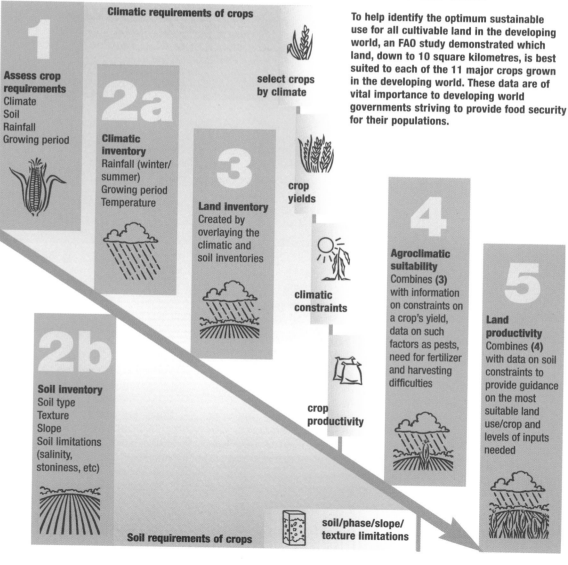

Climatic requirements of crops

1 Assess crop requirements
Climate
Soil
Rainfall
Growing period

2a Climatic inventory
Rainfall (winter/summer)
Growing period
Temperature

select crops by climate

3 Land inventory
Created by overlaying the climatic and soil inventories

crop yields

climatic constraints

crop productivity

4 Agroclimatic suitability
Combines (3) with information on constraints on a crop's yield, data on such factors as pests, need for fertilizer and harvesting difficulties

5 Land productivity
Combines (4) with data on soil constraints to provide guidance on the most suitable land use/crop and levels of inputs needed

2b Soil inventory
Soil type
Texture
Slope
Soil limitations (salinity, stoniness, etc)

Soil requirements of crops

soil/phase/slope/texture limitations

Fisheries at the limit?

Fishing is an important source of highly nutritious food, income and employment. Millions of people in Asia get most of their dietary protein from the aquatic harvest. In all, marine and inland fisheries provide nearly 30 percent of the region's animal protein; in Africa the proportion is 21 percent; in Latin America, 8 percent. About 30 percent of world production is turned into fishmeal to fatten livestock or farmed fish rather than eaten directly by humans.

About 60 percent of the world fish harvest is caught by developing countries where 100 million people depend on fishing and related industries for their livelihoods. By far the majority of world fish taken, some 85 percent, comes from the oceans. Although fish farming is gaining ground, fishing is still the main expression of man's ancient role as a hunter-gatherer.

Since 1950 the world fish catch, excluding aquaculture, has increased fivefold – rising from 20 million tonnes to peak at slightly less than 90 million tonnes in 1989. This period of expansion was made possible in large part by the introduction of new technologies and the spread of fishing fleets from traditional fishing areas to new ones, many of them in the southern hemisphere. No major commercial fish stock remains untouched. By the beginning of the 1990s, about 69 percent of the stocks for which data were available to FAO were either fully to heavily exploited (44 percent), overexploited (16 percent), depleted (6 percent) or very slowly recovering from overfishing (3 percent). As a result, the world catch has fallen in recent years although it now seems to be levelling off at around 85 million tonnes per year.

The world's fishing fleet has grown twice as fast as catches and there are now about 3.5 million vessels worldwide. Asia has the largest fleet with 42 percent of the total registered tonnage, followed by the republics of the former USSR with 30 percent. Africa has the smallest one at 2.7 percent. Government subsidies have helped keep most big fishing fleets afloat: in 1989 the world's 20 largest fishing nations paid out US$ 54 000 million in subsidies to catch US$ 70 000 million worth of fish. Such overcapacity has led to chronic overfishing with too many boats chasing too few fish.

Compared with other agricultural commodities, fish plays an important role as an earner of foreign exchange: net exports of fishery products by developing countries were more than US$ 11 000 million in 1993, much higher than coffee, bananas, rubber, tea, meat, rice or other typical commodities.

Contribution of fish to human diet, 1987-89
Fish as percentage of total animal protein intake

North America
6.6

Latin America and Caribbean
8.2

Western Europe
9.7

Africa
21.1

Near East
7.8

Far East
27.8

WORLD
16.0

Fish production and utilization

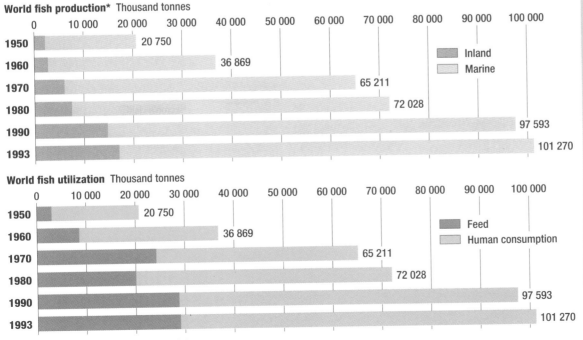

World fish production* Thousand tonnes

Year	Value
1950	20 750
1960	36 869
1970	65 211
1980	72 028
1990	97 593
1993	101 270

Inland / Marine

World fish utilization Thousand tonnes

Year	Value
1950	20 750
1960	36 869
1970	65 211
1980	72 028
1990	97 593
1993	101 270

Feed / Human consumption

*Including aquaculture production, excluding aquatic plants

Top ten fishing nations, 1993
Thousand tonnes

China
17 568

Japan
8 460

Peru
8 451

Chile
6 038

United States
5 939

Russian Federation
4 461

India
4 175

Indonesia
3 638

Thailand
3 348

Republic of Korea
2 649

Responsible fishing

Nearly 70 percent of the world's marine fish stocks are in trouble and urgently in need of conservation. Catches have collapsed in the Black Sea; less than 200 000 tonnes of fish were landed in 1991, compared to 1 million tonnes in the late 1980s. Stocks of bottom-living fish in the East China and Yellow Seas have fallen to between one-fifth and one-tenth of their highest levels. Other crisis areas include the Northwest and Northeast Atlantic, the North Sea, the Mediterranean and Black Seas, the Central Baltic, the Gulf of Thailand and the Western Central Pacific. Nearly all the inland fisheries of Asia and Africa also show signs of overexploitation.

Attempts to manage marine fisheries have generally failed. Instead conflicts have grown as stocks have fallen. Developed country fleets have clashed over fisheries in both the Northwest and Northeast Atlantic while large-scale commercial fleets are at odds with small-scale artisanal fishermen off many developing countries.

The international fishery commissions, established under the auspices of FAO (the first in 1948), have broadened the scope of management options and included many developing countries, but have so far had little success other than trying to impose quotas and regulate fishing gear and boat size. But they provide the mechanisms for sustainable fisheries management if countries would show the necessary cooperation and political will.

The third UN Convention on the Law of the Sea, which came into force in 1994, enables coastal states to establish exclusive economic zones, usually stretching 200 miles from their shores, where they have complete control of resources – providing a new opportunity for better regulation. In 1994 work started on drafting a Code of Conduct for Responsible Fisheries under the auspices of FAO, offering hope – if it is observed – of a new era in fisheries management.

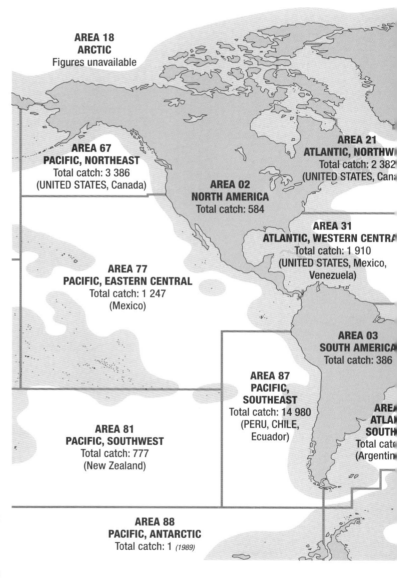

AREA 18
ARCTIC
Figures unavailable

AREA 67
PACIFIC, NORTHEAST
Total catch: 3 386
(UNITED STATES, Canada)

AREA 02
NORTH AMERICA
Total catch: 584

AREA 21
ATLANTIC, NORTHW
Total catch: 2 382
(UNITED STATES, Cana

AREA 31
ATLANTIC, WESTERN CENTRA
Total catch: 1 910
(UNITED STATES, Mexico, Venezuela)

AREA 77
PACIFIC, EASTERN CENTRAL
Total catch: 1 247
(Mexico)

AREA 03
SOUTH AMERICA
Total catch: 386

AREA 87
PACIFIC, SOUTHEAST
Total catch: 14 980
(PERU, CHILE, Ecuador)

AREA
ATLANTIC
SOUTH
Total cat
(Argentin

AREA 81
PACIFIC, SOUTHWEST
Total catch: 777
(New Zealand)

AREA 88
PACIFIC, ANTARCTIC
Total catch: 1 (1989)

INTERNATIONAL FISHERY COMMISSIONS (* FAO fishery body)

Pacific Ocean
North Pacific Marine Science Organization (PICES)
International North Pacific Fisheries Commission (INPFC)
Inter-American Tropical Tuna Commission (IATTC)
Council of the Eastern Pacific Tuna Fishing Agreement (CEPTFA)
Eastern Pacific Tuna Fishing Organization (OAPA)
South Pacific Permanent Commission (CPPS)

fishing zones

World fish catches, 1993
Fish and shellfish, thousand tonnes

▫ 200 nautical mile EEZ (exclusive economic zone)
— FAO fishing area boundary

Area numbers 01-07 refer to inland fisheries. All other area numbers refer to marine fisheries. Countries which caught over 200 000 tonnes within each marine FAO area are listed and those which caught over 1 million tonnes are shown in capitals.

AREA 27 ATLANTIC, NORTHEAST
Total catch: 10 788
MARK, ICELAND, NORWAY, United Kingdom,
an Federation, Spain, France, Netherlands,
, Ireland, Germany, Faeroe Islands, Portugal)

AREA 18 ARCTIC
Figures unavailable

AREA 07 AREA OF THE FORMER USSR
Total catch: 595

AREA 37 MEDITERRANEAN & BLACK SEA
Total catch: 1 670 (Turkey, Italy)

AREA 05 EUROPE
Total catch: 487

AREA 04 ASIA
Total catch: 13 300

AREA 61 PACIFIC, NORTHWEST
Total catch: 24 805
(CHINA, RUSSIAN FEDERATION, REPUBLIC OF KOREA, DEMOCRATIC PEOPLE'S REPUBLIC OF KOREA, Poland, Hong Kong)

34 TIC, EASTERN CENTRAL
atch: 2 941
, Morocco, Senegal, Ghana)

AREA 01 AFRICA
Total catch: 1 791

AREA 71 PACIFIC, WESTERN CENTRAL
Total catch: 8 374
(THAILAND, INDONESIA, PHILIPPINES, Viet Nam, Japan, Malaysia)

AREA 51 INDIAN OCEAN, WESTERN
Total catch: 3 834
(INDIA, Pakistan, Iran, Sri Lanka)

AREA 06 OCEANIA
Total catch: 22

AREA 47 ATLANTIC, SOUTHEAST
Total catch: 1 429
uth Africa, Namibia,
ussian Federation)

AREA 57 INDIAN OCEAN, EASTERN
Total catch: 3 466
(India, Thailand, Myanmar, Indonesia, Malaysia, Bangladesh)

AREA 81

AREA 48 TIC, ANTARCTIC
Total catch: 86

AREA 58 INDIAN OCEAN, ANTARCTIC
Total catch: 8

AREA 88

Top ten marine catches, 1993
Thousand tonnes

Anchoveta
8 300
Alaska pollack
4 758
Chilean jack mackerel
3 364
Japanese pilchard
2 306
Capelin
1 742
South American pilchard
1 624
Atlantic herring
1 613
Skipjack tuna
1 365
Atlantic cod
1 139
European pilchard
1 110

Total world catch, 1993

Top ten species
32 percent

All other species
68 percent

South Pacific Forum Fisheries Agency (FFA)
South Pacific Commission (SPC)

Atlantic Ocean and adjacent seas
International Council for the Exploration of the Sea (ICES)
North-East Atlantic Fisheries Commission (NEAFC)
North Atlantic Salmon Commission (NASCO)
Northwest Atlantic Fisheries Organization (NAFO)
General Fisheries Council for the Mediterranean (GFCM) *

Fishery Committee for the Eastern Central Atlantic (CECAF) *
Western Central Atlantic Fishery Commission (WECAFC) *
Regional Fisheries Advisory Commission for the Southwest Atlantic (CARPAS) *
International Commission for the Conservation of Atlantic Tunas (ICCAT)
International Commission for the Southeast Atlantic Fisheries (ICSEAF)

Indian Ocean and Indo-Pacific area
Indian Ocean Tuna Commission (IOTC) *
Indian Ocean Fishery Commission (IOFC) *
Indo-Pacific Fishery Commission (IPFC) *

Other areas
International Whaling Commission (IWC)
Latin American Organization for the Development of Fisheries (OLDEPESCA)
Commission for the Conservation of Antarctic Marine Living Resources (CCAMLR)
Commission for Inland Fisheries of Latin America (COPESCAL) *
European Inland Fisheries Advisory Commission (EIFAC) *
Committee for Inland Fisheries of Africa (CIFA) *
Advisory Committee on Fisheries Research (ACFR)

Aquaculture: From hunter to farmer

Aquaculture is the farming of aquatic organisms, including fish, molluscs, crustaceans and aquatic plants. The proportion of world total fish production derived from aquaculture doubled in less than a decade from 8 percent in 1984 to 16 percent in 1993.

Seaweed harvest, India (above).
Carp farm, China (right).
Carp (far right).

People have been farming fish for thousands of years. The Chinese raised fish in ponds some 3 000 years ago; the Romans farmed oysters in shallow coastal bays; and mediaeval monks in Europe reared fish on table scraps in ponds fertilized with human waste.

Today aquaculture has become big business in Asia, Latin America, North America and Europe. Smaller-scale activities, raising fish in village ponds, also take place in some sub-Saharan African countries and in Asia, while Thai, Indonesian, Chinese, Malaysian and Filippino farmers also farm fish in rice paddies for their own consumption.

These enterprises – whether in large ponds, in sea cages or in tiny backyard ponds – hold much promise for meeting increasing food demands. In fact, with most capture fisheries in decline, aquaculture is the best way to maintain and increase supplies of saltwater and freshwater fish.

Fish farming expanded greatly between 1984 and 1993, growing at an average rate of 9 percent a year. In 1993, aquaculture produced 22.6 million tonnes of fish, shellfish, invertebrates and plants (mostly seaweed), worth US$ 35 708 million. It contributes 16 percent to global fisheries production, compared to just over 8 percent in 1984. Over half of all freshwater fish production comes from aquaculture.

Asia accounted for nearly 87 percent of the world's fish farming output in 1993: 63 percent of its share was produced by China, with India as the next biggest contributor.

The industry is overwhelmingly concentrated in the developing world, which accounts for 85 percent of output by volume and 71 percent by value. Exports of high-value species such as shrimp, prawns and salmon earn much-needed foreign currency for these countries. Fish farming may increasingly be the only way for some poor communities, who rely on fish and shellfish for the bulk of their protein intake, to maintain a healthy diet.

In spite of this promise, aquaculture projects are vulnerable to disease and environmental problems. Overstocking and pollution have devastated some Asian

The growth of aquaculture

Finfish, crustaceans and molluscs, million tonnes

■ Inland aquaculture   ■ Marine aquaculture

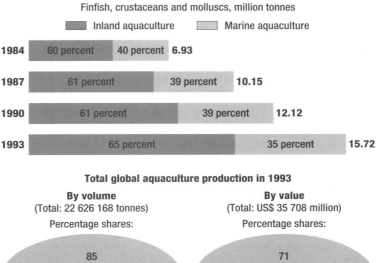

	Inland aquaculture	Marine aquaculture	Total
1984	60 percent	40 percent	6.93
1987	61 percent	39 percent	10.15
1990	61 percent	39 percent	12.12
1993	65 percent	35 percent	15.72

Total global aquaculture production in 1993

By volume
(Total: 22 626 168 tonnes)
Percentage shares:

85
15

By value
(Total: US$ 35 708 million)
Percentage shares:

71
29

■ Developing countries   ■ Industrialized countries

Fish provides 17 percent of the world's animal protein; in some countries the figure is as high as 50 percent. With the fish harvest from the wild now dangerously overstretched we may have to depend increasingly upon aquaculture to meet demand for fish in the future.

Top eleven aquaculture producers, 1993
Tonnes

China
8 880 167
India
1 438 915
Japan
833 032
Indonesia
592 081
United States
433 698
Thailand
414 269
Philippines
391 703
Republic of Korea
391 424
France
270 880
Bangladesh
247 816
Viet Nam
192 000

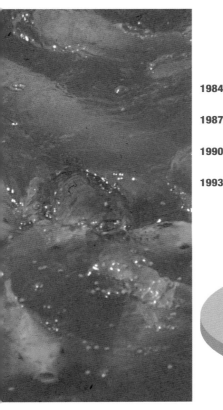

and Latin American freshwater operations. Marine aquaculture is constrained by the rising pollution of coastal waters. Nutrient and organic over-enrichment, the accumulation of toxic chemicals, microbial contamination, siltation and sedimentation all jeopardize expansion. Where aquaculture results in the degradation of coastal mangroves, the breeding grounds of many wild species, it poses a major threat to biological diversity.

Better selection of production sites to safeguard the environment and sound management techniques can overcome most of these difficulties. FAO expects aquaculture's output to double in volume within the next 15 years.

Inland fisheries and aquaculture

The cultivation of **carp** has a long tradition, particularly in Europe and Asia. They still dominate aquaculture, accounting for most of the fish production. For home ponds they have the advantage of being non-carnivorous and so not requiring expensive protein-rich foods.

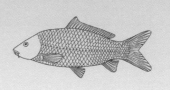

Tilapia, the mainstay of small-scale aquaculture for many poor farmers, have spread far from their original African home. Dubbed "the aquatic chicken" they are most widely farmed in Asia, particularly China, the Philippines and Thailand.

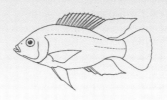

About half of the annual harvest of **shrimp** – a high value export product – comes from aquaculture. Progress in the production of shrimp over the past 10 years has been largely responsible for a fourfold increase in the annual harvest of crustaceans.

Forests of the world

Forest types
(top to bottom):
boreal, Finland;
temperate rainforest,
United States;
tropical rainforest,
Venezuela;
tropical dry, Australia;
temperate dry, Poland.

The world's forests cover some 3 400 million hectares – an area the size of North and South America combined. They are sources of raw materials and food, and are essential for maintaining agricultural productivity and the environmental well-being of the planet as a whole.

Trees and forests anchor the soil and buffer the winds, thus protecting against erosion by wind and water. They produce oxygen and absorb carbon dioxide, the major agent in global warming. They intercept rainfall, releasing it slowly into soils, surface waters and underground aquifers. The water vapour released from their foliage in transpiration influences climate and is a vital part of the hydrological cycle.

Forests and woodlands vary from the dense rainforests of the tropics to East Africa's open woodland savannahs; from mangroves to the mixed temperate broadleaved and boreal forests. But unmanaged harvesting, ill-planned clearance for farming, or physiological pressures from pollution can pose a threat to any forest type.

During the 1980s more than 15 million hectares of tropical forests were lost each year: the overwhelming majority of the deforestation was intended to provide land for agriculture. The largest losses occurred in tropical moist deciduous forests, the areas best suited for settlement and farming. The extent of these forests declined by 61 million hectares – more than 10 percent of their area – while 46 million hectares, or 60 percent, of tropical rainforests were lost. Few of these areas have been replanted.

Tree cover is increasing in many temperate regions, mainly due to the establishment of forest plantations. Europe increased its forest and wooded land by 2 percent over the 1980s and there were small increases in New Zealand and Australia. In the same decade, however, a drop of some 3.5 million hectares occurred in the United States. The area of the former USSR reported an increase between 1978 and 1988. However, there is an urgent need to bring many of the Siberian forests under

sustainable management to avoid their degradation. As well as managing some forests for production, diversity should be preserved in others by designating protected areas.

Many forests in industrialized countries have been damaged by airborne pollutants, including acid rain: the International Institute for Applied Systems Analysis (IIASA) has estimated that US$ 60 000 million would have to be spent annually for 25 years to protect Europe's forests from pollution.

Global distribution of forests

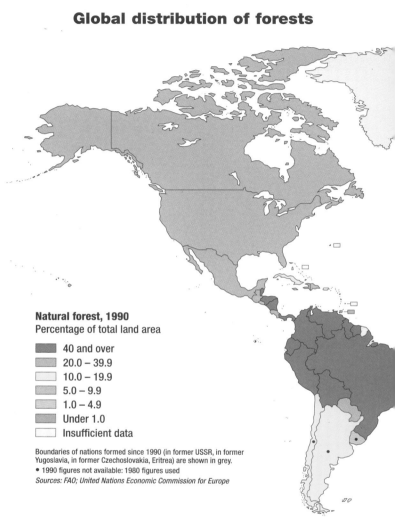

Natural forest, 1990
Percentage of total land area

- 40 and over
- 20.0 – 39.9
- 10.0 – 19.9
- 5.0 – 9.9
- 1.0 – 4.9
- Under 1.0
- Insufficient data

Boundaries of nations formed since 1990 (in former USSR, in former Yugoslavia, in former Czechoslovakia, Eritrea) are shown in grey.
● 1990 figures not available: 1980 figures used
Sources: FAO; United Nations Economic Commission for Europe

PROTECT AND PRODUCE DIMENSIONS OF NEED

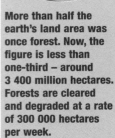

Where the forests are

- Boreal forest
- Temperate forest
- Tropical forest

Source: World Conservation Monitoring Centre

More than half the earth's land area was once forest. Now, the figure is less than one-third – around 3 400 million hectares. Forests are cleared and degraded at a rate of 300 000 hectares per week.

Projected uses and speed of destruction

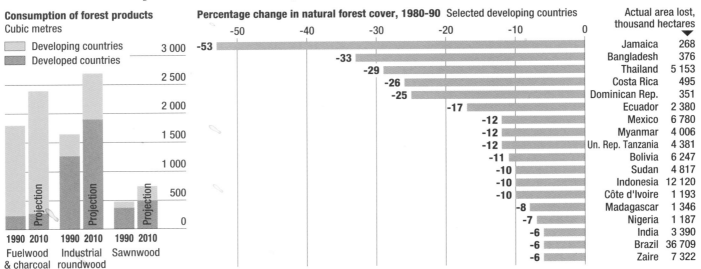

Consumption of forest products
Cubic metres

- Developing countries
- Developed countries

1990 2010	1990 2010	1990 2010
Fuelwood & charcoal	Industrial roundwood	Sawnwood

Percentage change in natural forest cover, 1980-90 Selected developing countries

Actual area lost, thousand hectares

Country	% change	Actual area lost
Jamaica	-53	268
Bangladesh	-33	376
Thailand	-29	5 153
Costa Rica	-26	495
Dominican Rep.	-25	351
Ecuador	-17	2 380
Mexico	-12	6 780
Myanmar	-12	4 006
Un. Rep. Tanzania	-12	4 381
Bolivia	-11	6 247
Sudan	-10	4 817
Indonesia	-10	12 120
Côte d'Ivoire	-10	1 193
Madagascar	-8	1 346
Nigeria	-7	1 187
India	-6	3 390
Brazil	-6	36 709
Zaire	-6	7 322

Wealth from the wild

Harvesting wild resources (from the top): fishing in mangrove forest, Viet Nam; collecting honey, Senegal; tapping rubber, Thailand; gathering mushrooms, Nepal.

Forest lands offer a wealth of products other than wood, that benefit both rural communities and humanity as a whole.

Three-quarters of the world's people use folk medicines derived largely from forest plants and animals, while the Worldwatch Institute estimates that more than US$ 100 000 million worth of drugs with active ingredients developed from the forests are sold worldwide each year.

Meat from wild animals may be a major source of protein for many remote villages. Leaves, bark and seeds supplement diets, providing vitamins and trace minerals, while genes from forest plants are used to boost agricultural yields around the world.

Global trade in forest products, other than wood, runs into thousands of millions of dollars annually. In the state of Manipur, India, for example, 90 percent of the people depend on them as a major source of income.

Animal products

By conservative estimates wild animals provide more than three-quarters of dietary protein in Zaire. The world's 240 000 square kilometres of coastal mangrove forests provide vital nursery, feeding and breeding grounds for commercially valuable fish and shellfish including, for example, nearly 90 percent of the commercial catch in the Gulf of Mexico.

Insects are rich in vitamins and minerals: bee larvae contain ten times more vitamin D than fish-liver oil. Honey supports an important forest industry, as well as providing a particularly nutritious food: Indian villages are estimated to produce more than 37 000 tonnes of it a year. And a drug obtained from the saliva of leeches is used worldwide in skin transplants, and to treat rheumatism and thrombosis.

The glands of the musk deer are used to make perfume, while the tree iguanas of Latin America are farmed for both their meat and their skins, which are sold to make belts, watch bands and shoes.

Plant products

More than 6 000 forest plants have long been used as natural medicines, and many have become the basis for modern pharmaceuticals. The rosy periwinkle, from the forests of Madagascar, has revolutionized the chances of children surviving leukemia. Taxol, from the western yew in northwestern American forests, is one of the most potent anti-cancer drugs ever found.

The sago palm is a staple food for more than 300 000 people in Melanesia; the 700 000 people of the Upper Shaba area of Zaire consume 20 tonnes of mushrooms every year. Genes from wild forest species have been used to improve wheat, sugar, coffee and many other crops and to protect them from devastating outbreaks of disease.

Exports of rattan and of palm nuts and kernels are worth more than US$ 2 000 million a year, and some 1.5 million people in the Brazilian Amazon get much of their income from harvesting rubber and other forest products.

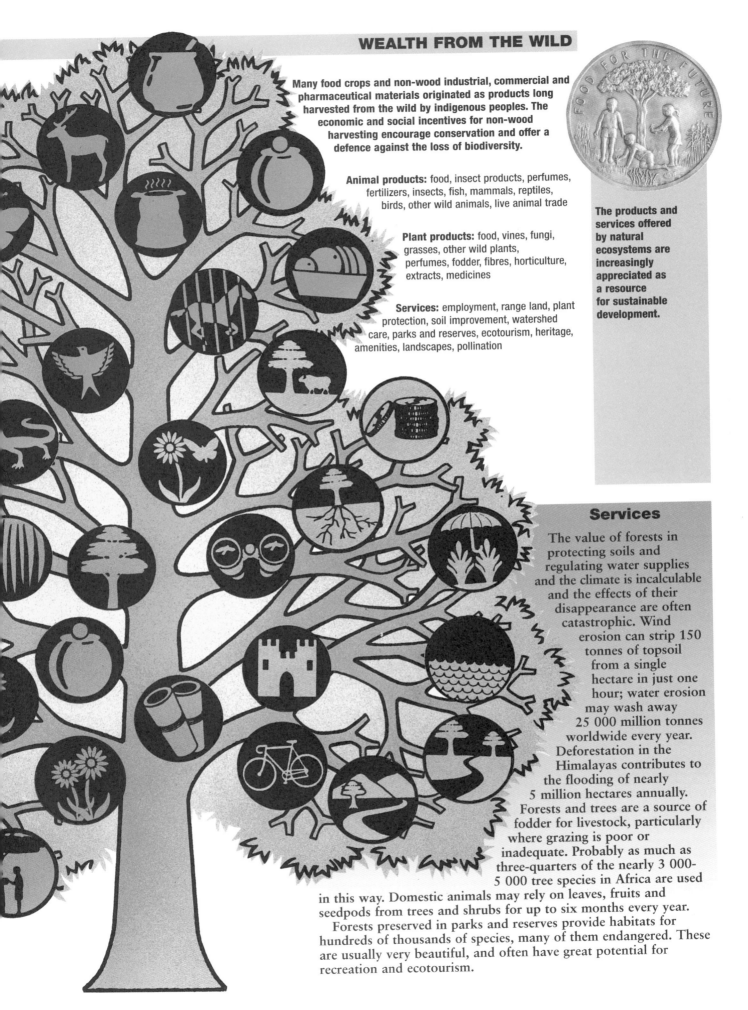

WEALTH FROM THE WILD

Many food crops and non-wood industrial, commercial and pharmaceutical materials originated as products long harvested from the wild by indigenous peoples. The economic and social incentives for non-wood harvesting encourage conservation and offer a defence against the loss of biodiversity.

Animal products: food, insect products, perfumes, fertilizers, insects, fish, mammals, reptiles, birds, other wild animals, live animal trade

Plant products: food, vines, fungi, grasses, other wild plants, perfumes, fodder, fibres, horticulture, extracts, medicines

Services: employment, range land, plant protection, soil improvement, watershed care, parks and reserves, ecotourism, heritage, amenities, landscapes, pollination

The products and services offered by natural ecosystems are increasingly appreciated as a resource for sustainable development.

Services

The value of forests in protecting soils and regulating water supplies and the climate is incalculable and the effects of their disappearance are often catastrophic. Wind erosion can strip 150 tonnes of topsoil from a single hectare in just one hour; water erosion may wash away 25 000 million tonnes worldwide every year. Deforestation in the Himalayas contributes to the flooding of nearly 5 million hectares annually. Forests and trees are a source of fodder for livestock, particularly where grazing is poor or inadequate. Probably as much as three-quarters of the nearly 3 000-5 000 tree species in Africa are used in this way. Domestic animals may rely on leaves, fruits and seedpods from trees and shrubs for up to six months every year.

Forests preserved in parks and reserves provide habitats for hundreds of thousands of species, many of them endangered. These are usually very beautiful, and often have great potential for recreation and ecotourism.

What are forests worth?

Forests are usually worth much more left standing than when they are cut down. Studies in Peru, the Brazilian Amazon, the Philippines and Indonesia suggest that harvesting forest products sustainably is at least twice as profitable as clearing them for timber or to provide land for agriculture.

A study in Peru showed that sustainably harvesting forest products from just 1 hectare of forest could be worth US$ 422 annually, year after year.

Cutting down and selling the timber from the same hectare would yield a one-time return of US$ 1 000.

Another study in Palawan, the Philippines, showed that coastal fisheries could earn local fishermen US$ 28 million a year if forests on the island's watershed were left intact, thus preserving the coral reef upon which the fisheries were based. As it happened, the trees were cut, the resulting soil erosion killed the reef and the fisheries disappeared.

People and wildlife

Wildlife conservation is generally most effective when local people benefit from it; when they are hostile, there is little chance of effective protection. Wildlife reserves often try to keep local people out, denying them the chance to make a living from the land, while elephants, tigers and other large animals often trample crops or kill livestock and people in areas adjacent to them.

Policies and protected areas are increasingly being designed to attract local support. Quotas have been set for hunting antelope in Zambia's Kafue Flats wetlands. The local people decide how many to kill themselves and how many to reserve for trophy hunting tourists at US$ 500 a time: under this regime, the antelope, threatened by poaching before the change of policy, have flourished and increased. Zimbabwe has also introduced trophy hunting, at high prices, and ploughs the money back into conservation and local communities.

Protected areas in Papua New Guinea are often run by local committees, and the people are given incentives to exploit the forest sustainably, such as through butterfly farming. Game ranching also holds promise for conservation. In New Zealand, some 4 500 farmers manage forested rangeland, yielding more than US$ 26 million a year in exports.

For animal populations to flourish, local people must benefit from protected areas.

Many benefits follow when forests are conserved:
• protection of wild species which could provide future crops, medicines or industrial raw materials;
• prevention of erosion, conservation of water resources and stabilization of local climates;
• the safeguarding of productive wild resources and encouragement of tourism.

Trekking in Himalayan mountain forest, Nepal (left).

Ecotourism

Ecotourism is one of the fastest growing areas of the tourism industry. It is estimated to be increasing by some 10-15 percent a year.

Two-fifths of visitors to Costa Rica – one of the pioneers of ecotourism – now come to see its forests, landscape and wildlife.

The environment and tourists both gain from game reserves such as these in Latin America and Africa.

Ecotourists in South Florida are thought to spend almost US$ 2 000 million a year and trips to Antarctica increased four-fold in as many years in the early 1990s.

Ecotourism offers an important opportunity to earn many millions of dollars per year from conservation. But ecotourists can end up damaging the very wild areas they have come to admire. Coral reefs around the world have been ruined by visitors. The lodges in one village on the Nepalese hiker trails fell a hectare of forest every year, causing more than 30 tonnes of soil to be eroded away.

Experts say that the effects of ecotourism should be monitored and the industry regulated if it is to achieve its potential for conservation. Small-scale operations are usually the most benign, but only a few, like the Toledo Ecotourism Association in Costa Rica, are run by local villagers.

Controlling pests

Tsetse fly

Screwworm fly

Black tarantula

Pests and diseases have no regard for national borders. FAO's EMPRES programme is a major initiative for transboundary control of pests.

Pests cost thousands of millions of dollars annually in lost agricultural production, and at least 10 percent of the world's harvest is destroyed, mainly by rodents and insects, while in storage. In 1970 disease devastated one-sixth of the United States' maize crop. Later that decade, Java lost 70 percent of its rice crop to brown planthoppers, while a 1976 outbreak of New World screwworm in Texas cost US$ 375 million. The world's potato farmers spend some US$ 1 600 million annually to combat the fungus that caused the Irish potato famine of the 1840s. Rinderpest, a killer disease which in the 1890s wiped out 80-90 percent of all cattle in sub-Saharan Africa is now the target of a coordinated Pan-African eradication campaign.

Pesticides help. Their use multiplied by a factor of 32 between 1950 and 1986, with developing countries now accounting for a quarter of the world's pesticide use. But inappropriate and excessive use can cause contamination of both food and environment and, in some cases, damage the health of farmers.

Pesticides also kill the natural enemies of pests, allowing them to multiply; meanwhile the number of pest species with resistance to pesticides has increased from a handful 50 years ago to over 700 now.

Biological controls, such as the use of pests' natural enemies, are useful. In West Africa, the introduction of a wasp has brought about a spectacular control of the mealybug, thereby saving cassava, the basic food crop for millions of Africans. In India the seeds of the neem tree (*Azadirachta indica*) are used as a natural insecticide to protect crops and stored grain. Researchers have found that the active compounds can control over 200 species of pest, including major pests such as locusts, maize borers and rice weevils, yet do not harm birds, mammals or beneficial insects such as bees.

Scientists have developed new varieties of plants, often using genes from wild varieties with inbuilt disease resistance. Genes from the wild have been used to protect Brazil's coffee plantations, while a Mexican wild maize confers resistance to seven major diseases.

Both pesticides and biological controls can be expensive: pests become increasingly resistant to chemicals, and the genetic resistance of plants to pests needs to be renewed regularly by the plant breeder. Integrated pest management (IPM), now the basis of FAO plant protection activities, combines a variety of controls, including the conservation of existing natural enemies, crop rotation, intercropping, and the use of pest-resistant varieties. Pesticides may still continue to be used selectively but in much smaller quantities.

Five years after IPM was widely introduced in Indonesia, rice yields increased by 13 percent, while pesticide use dropped by 60 percent; in the first two years alone the Government saved US$ 120 million that it would have spent subsidizing the chemicals. In the Sudan, IPM produced good results with a more than 50 percent reduction in insecticide use. In the United States, a 1987 study found that apple growers in New York state and almond growers in California who used IPM substantially increased their yields.

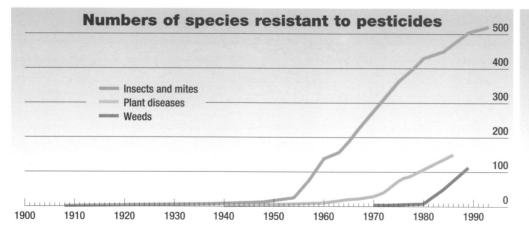

Numbers of species resistant to pesticides

— Insects and mites
— Plant diseases
— Weeds

1900 1910 1920 1930 1940 1950 1960 1970 1980 1990

0 100 200 300 400 500

Pesticide safety

FAO keeps countries informed of pesticides that are generally acceptabl and helps to ensure that pesticides are properly labelled and packaged. It is a eliciting support for the destruction of large stocks of hazardous pesticides th have built up in many developing countries. Most developing countries have neither the resources nor the expertise to rid themselves of these to and useless chemicals. FAO puts the quantity of obsolete pesticides in Afric alone at 20 000-30 000 tonnes, which will cost up to US$ 150 million to destr

Worldwide locust distribution

Pests threaten crops, livestock and humans. At least 520 insects and mites, 150 plant diseases and 113 weeds have become resistant to pesticides meant to control them.

Severe locust plagues in 1987-89 were mainly fought with chemical pesticides. Since then, environmental concerns have necessitated the development of alternative strategies.

Desert locusts (*Schistocerca gregaria*) have swept over Africa, the Middle East and western Asia for millennia. Under particularly favourable breeding conditions numbers can reach plague proportions. Often assisted by winds, swarms of 400 million or more insects, each one able to eat its own weight in vegetation every day, travel great distances at bewildering speed, and can strip entire areas of crops.

FAO began its Locust Control Programme in 1952, and has been at the centre of attempts to combat outbreaks ever since. It runs the Desert Locust Information Service which provides early warning to affected countries and international donors.

In 1994 FAO set up the Emergency Prevention System for Transboundary Animal and Plant Pests and Diseases (EMPRES); its initial priorities were to improve management of desert locusts and eradicate

rinderpest worldwide. It looks at ways to target locusts without affecting other life, including non-chemical means.

Change in pesticide use

	-100	-50	0	50	100	150	200	250	300	350	400
Myanmar										+382 (357)	
Oman							+203 (569)				
Islamic Rep. of Iran					+92 (25 917)						
Malaysia				+61 (44 721)							
Pakistan			+24 (5 518)								
Cyprus		-15 (1 679)									
Sweden		-38 (1 467)									
Finland		-39 (1 353)									
Romania		-58 (13 134)									
Egypt		-65 (5 550)									
Hungary		-67 (11 402)									
Cameroon		-69 (1 292)									

Percentage change, selected countries, 1989-92. Figures in brackets show total pesticide use 1992, in tonnes.

International statistics on pesticide use are incomplete. This chart shows some recent trends. The volume of use varies greatly and many developing countries may have to increase pesticide use if they are to increase their agricultural production. Some countries, including Indonesia, the Netherlands and Sweden, are committed to reducing use.

Biological diversity

1.4-1.75 million species have been identified but scientists believe that there are over 13.5 million more species. The size of the grey drawings indicates the number of species known, while the larger shadow indicates the total estimated number.

The diversity of life on earth is essential to the survival of humanity. Yet it is being lost at an unprecedented rate. Natural habitats are being destroyed, degraded and depleted, resulting in the loss of countless wild species. Traditional crop varieties and animal breeds are being replaced with new ones that are more suited to modern agriculture.

When natural diversity is lost, so is irreplaceable genetic material, the essential building blocks of the plants and animals on which agriculture depends. These plants and animals are the result of 3 000 million years of natural evolution – and 12 000 years of domestication and selection. Of the thousands of plant species that can be used for food, only 15-20 are of major economic importance. In fact, only a handful supply the dietary energy needs of most of the world's population. Since 1900, however, about 75 percent of the genetic diversity of agricultural crops has been lost.

In India, there will soon only be 30-50 rice varieties covering an area where 30 000 once flourished. Half of the animal breeds that existed in Europe at the start of the present century are now extinct, and one-quarter of the livestock breeds in the rest of the world are now at high risk of loss. The traditional knowledge and skills of indigenous peoples – who selected, bred and cultivated such varieties over thousands of years – are also disappearing, often along with the people themselves.

The loss of genetic resources has accelerated with the spread of intensive agriculture and high-yielding crop varieties to large parts of the developing world, replacing the traditional diversity of crops with monocultures. Yet the varieties being lost may contain genes that could be used to develop even more productive varieties or to improve resistance to pests. The N'Dama cattle of West Africa, for example, have developed tolerance, over thousands of years, to trypanosomiasis, which threatens some 160 million other domesticated animals in Africa, costing an estimated US$ 5 000 million a year in meat production alone.

Popular movements to conserve traditional crop varieties are spreading throughout the world. The Seed Savers Exchange, a network of around 1 000 farmers and gardeners in the United States, locates and conserves thousands of varieties of endangered vegetables. KENGO, a network group in Kenya, promotes the conservation and use of indigenous tree species.

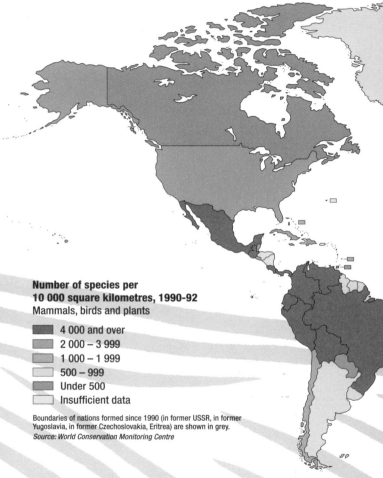

Number of species per 10 000 square kilometres, 1990-92
Mammals, birds and plants

- ■ 4 000 and over
- ■ 2 000 – 3 999
- ■ 1 000 – 1 999
- □ 500 – 999
- ■ Under 500
- □ Insufficient data

Boundaries of nations formed since 1990 (in former USSR, in former Yugoslavia, in former Czechoslovakia, Eritrea) are shown in grey.
Source: World Conservation Monitoring Centre

ANIMAL GENETIC RESOURCES

The cost of conserving biodiversity is less than the penalty of allowing its destruction. Once lost, this heritage cannot be recovered.

Number of species by area

Domesticated animals at risk

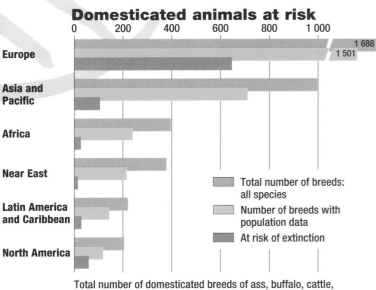

	0	200	400	600	800	1 000
Europe						1 688 / 1 501
Asia and Pacific						
Africa						
Near East						
Latin America and Caribbean						
North America						

Total number of breeds: all species
Number of breeds with population data
At risk of extinction

Total number of domesticated breeds of ass, buffalo, cattle, goat, horse, pig and sheep

FAO stresses the importance of building the capacity of developing countries to conserve, develop and use diversity sustainably as a means of reducing hunger and poverty. The Organization has pioneered the concept of Farmers' Rights which recognizes that farmers and rural communities, especially those in the developing world, should be rewarded – and to no lesser extent than plant breeders – for the contribution they make to the creation, conservation and availability of genetic resources.

Sustainable agriculture and rural development

The challenges of increasing food production are daunting. Despite great agricultural advances, millions go hungry or live under threat of famine. Food production will have to double between 1995 and the year 2025 if the expected population of up to 8 500 million is to be fed adequately.

Parallel with population growth is the impact of pollution and the degradation of natural resources that threaten to limit gains in production and imperil sustainable agriculture. Achieving sustainable agriculture and rural development (SARD) will not be easy. Most of the best agricultural land is already under cultivation. The rate of expansion of cropland fell from 1 percent a year during the 1950s to 0.3 percent by the 1970s: by 1990 it was virtually at a standstill. Per caput water availability is also falling rapidly. Future increases in production depend mainly on increasing the productivity of existing agricultural land and water resources.

Farmer involvement is the key to sustainable agriculture. Given the right incentives and government support, farm families can and are making significant progress towards managing their land and water sustainably.

Some traditional farming systems using low inputs have improved yields while safeguarding the resource base. Indonesian rice farmers who adopted integrated pest management (IPM), which reduces the need for pesticides, soon achieved higher yields than those who relied solely on pesticides.

A diversity of crops or varieties can help protect farmers against failure. In a single Amazon community in Peru 168 different species of plants are cultivated. Small-scale potato growers in the Andes grow up to 100 distinct varieties, with a typical household growing 10-12.

Agricultural systems, in both developed and developing countries, need to use new approaches to increase food supplies while protecting the resources on which they depend. This can be achieved with practices that:
● fully exploit natural processes such as recycling nutrients, using plants that fix their own nitrogen and achieving a balance between pests and predators;
● reduce the reliance on inputs such as mineral fertilizers and chemical pesticides;
● diversify farming systems, making greater use of the biological and genetic potential of plant and animal species;
● improve the management of natural resources;
● rotate crops or develop agroforestry systems that help maintain soil fertility.

The ultimate objective should be the optimum mix of agricultural practices, both old and new, in order to maximize sustainable output within the limits of available resources.

The genes of wild animals such as the gaur (top) and jungle fowl (bottom) can be used to "refresh" the gene base of livestock.

Land

◻ Areas of air pollution: emissions leading to acid rain

▨ Sensitive soils / potential problem areas

▨ Present problem areas (including lakes and rivers)

Sea

▨ Areas of persistent coastal pollution

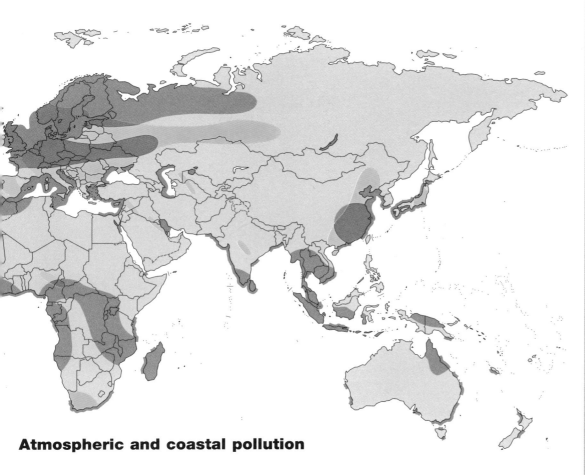

Atmospheric and coastal pollution

In the future, growth in food production will depend largely on finding ways to increase the productivity of existing agricultural land.

Old varieties represent a valuable gene bank that can be utilized to create improved crops. Potatoes, Peru (top) and apples, France (bottom).

Essential ingredients for sustainable development

Biological Continued conservation of genetic resources is essential if food supplies are to be increased. Authorities in regions rich in genetic resources should be encouraged to conserve wild species of animals and plants.

Physical Soil and water must be conserved to sustain plant productivity. This requires the introduction of land management to reduce or halt topsoil erosion and to maintain or increase the water-holding capacity of soil. Irrigated agriculture needs to be overhauled where water is wasted or crop yields are declining as a result of soil salinity and waterlogging. Atmospheric pollution, including acid rain, harms crops and forest stands. Excessive use of chemical fertilizers and pesticides poisons soils and reduces productivity.

Social Clear property rights and land tenure systems provide powerful incentives for owners and tenants to use their land in a sustainable way. Land tenure systems need reform in countries where land distribution is grossly unfair or where laws are inadequate to control land use, protect forests and safeguard rangelands. Participation must also be encouraged by local controls over planning and the allocation of resources.

Economic Farmers in developing countries need fair prices for their produce and better agricultural infrastructure, including adequate extension services and efficient transport for getting their food to markets. They need incentives to conserve soil and water resources.

The FAO definition of sustainable agricultural development is "the management and conservation of the natural resource base, and the orientation of technological and institutional change in such a manner as to ensure the attainment and continued satisfaction of human needs for present and future generations. Such development... conserves land, water, plant and animal genetic resources, is environmentally non-degrading, technically appropriate, economically viable and socially acceptable."

Agenda 21

Agenda 21 is the action plan adopted by leaders from 169 countries who met at the 1992 UN Conference on Environment and Development (UNCED) – generally referred to as the Earth Summit – in Rio de Janeiro. The action plan devotes a chapter to sustainable agriculture and rural development, which lays down that "major adjustments are needed in agricultural, environmental and macroeconomic policy, at both national and international levels, in developed as well as developing countries, to create the conditions for sustainable agriculture and rural development."

Sustainable development considerations, it says, must be integrated with agricultural analysis in all countries, not just developing ones, and notes that at present there is a "widespread absence" of such coherent national policy frameworks. Governments, it urges, should have sound policies in place by the turn of the century.

Agenda 21 puts priority on maintaining and improving the productivity of the best lands in order to support an expanding population. But, at the same time, the less good lands should be conserved and rehabilitated and further encroachment on marginal land should be avoided.

It provides detailed proposals in 12 policy areas. These include land reform and encouraging people to invest in the land by being provided with ownership, finance and the means to market their produce at fair prices. People should be trained in how to conserve the soil, combining the best contributions of both modern and traditional techniques. There should be better conservation of genetic resources. The benefits of plant breeding should be shared between those who provide and those who use the raw materials for it. And integrated pest management and plant nutrition should be widely adopted.

Elements for sustainable agriculture and rural development

INTEGRATED ACTIVITIES	KEY NATURAL RESOURCES	KEY EXTERNAL INPUTS
Government level: policies, instruments, development plans, agrarian reform, nutrition surveys, food quality and food security, data, monitoring, early warning systems	**Land:** land use planning, land management, soil conservation, land rehabilitation	**Pest management:** programmes and projects on integrated pest control, control of pesticide use
Rural community level: development of local organizations and capacity building for people's participation, training, extension	**Water:** water conservation, irrigation improvements, water database development, water-users' associations	**Plant nutrition:** programmes and projects for integrated plant nutrition
Area level: for example, coastal zones, watersheds, river basins, agro-ecological zones	**Plant and animal biological resources:** conservation of genetic resources, development of varieties and breeds	**Rural energy:** national strategies and technology transfer for integrated rural energy development
Production unit level: farming systems, diversification to increase incomes, creation of rural industries, credit and marketing	**Trees and forests:** reduction of deforestation rates, sustainable forest management and wood harvesting, promotion of non-wood forest uses and industries, conservation of habitats, integrating trees in farming systems	
Consumer level: improving nutrition and food quality, adjusting dietary patterns, product marketing	**Fisheries:** reduction of fishing effort to maximize production, increasing aquaculture production, exploitation of new species	

Building the
Global
Community

Dimensions of Need

A family of nations: 'Haves' and 'have nots'

Inequality and instability often go hand in hand.

There is a narrowing gap in terms of human survival, but still a widening one in some measures of quality of life such as incomes and years of schooling.

Income disparity between the richest 20 percent and the poorest 20 percent of the world's population
Ratio of income shares, richest : poorest

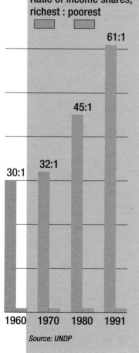

Source: UNDP

Gaps in human development

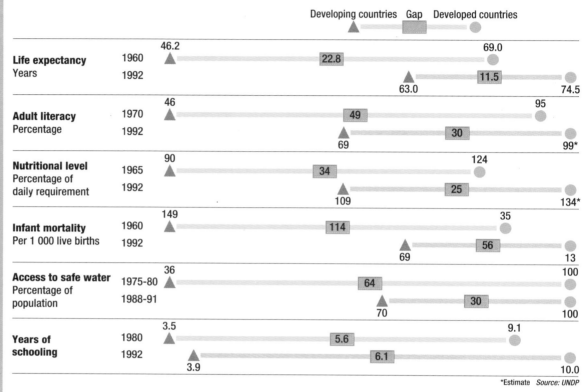

Estimate   Source: UNDP

The world, as a whole, is getting steadily wealthier. Global income has increased seven-fold over the past 50 years while income per person has more than tripled. But this wealth is poorly distributed. By the early 1990s, about 20 percent of the world's population – most of it in the developed world – received over 80 percent of the world's income, while the poorest 20 percent received only 1.4 percent. The developed countries consume 70 percent of the world's energy, 75 percent of its metals, 85 percent of its wood and 60 percent of its food.

In the developing world, the people spend a higher proportion of their small incomes on food than their counterparts in the industrialized countries. Food supplies tend to be unpredictable and nutrition poor. Jobs are scarce. Investment in education, health and sanitation is low. In some developing countries per caput income is falling. It fell on average by 2.4 percent a year in Haiti in the 1980s, in Zaire by 1.3 percent and in Mozambique by 1.1 percent. Per caput food production fell during the 1980s in at least 58 countries: by 1990, food availability was lower than total calorie needs in more than 40 developing countries.

Some of the gaps between rich and poor nations have narrowed since the 1960s, others have grown, but life expectancy is low and child mortality remains high in the poorest countries.

Developing nations often lack the institutions and mechanisms to redistribute their income. Unequal income distribution means that the top fifth of the population may receive as much as 25 times the income of the bottom fifth. Domestic policies are often biased in favour of urban populations: on average, rural communities, while still the majority in most developing countries, receive less than half the educational, health, water and sanitary services.

Global and national inequalities encourage migration and can create social unrest. An unequal world is an unstable world.

World trade:
Why is it important?

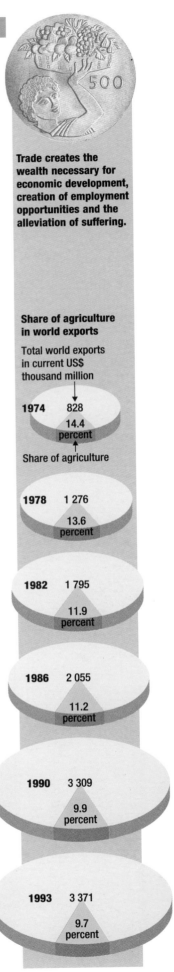

Trade creates the wealth necessary for economic development, creation of employment opportunities and the alleviation of suffering.

Share of agriculture in world exports

Total world exports in current US$ thousand million

| 1974 | 828 |
| | 14.4 percent |

Share of agriculture

| 1978 | 1 276 |
| | 13.6 percent |

| 1982 | 1 795 |
| | 11.9 percent |

| 1986 | 2 055 |
| | 11.2 percent |

| 1990 | 3 309 |
| | 9.9 percent |

| 1993 | 3 371 |
| | 9.7 percent |

Some US$ 3 800 000 million worth of goods were traded among the world's countries in 1993. Ideally, trade consists of one country selling what it is best able to produce, and buying what others produce better. It creates wealth which can be used to reduce poverty, generate income, create employment and develop the economy.

Trade is generally more effective than aid as an engine of development. If all things were equal, international trade would represent developing countries' best means of raising the funds necessary to meet their peoples' needs. But in reality the balance of trade is tilted against them.

Some developing countries are becoming more industrialized, but most of them still bring raw materials, or materials that have been little processed, such as minerals, timber and agricultural products, to the world marketplace. Raw materials provide nearly 90 percent of the export earnings of sub-Saharan African countries.

FAO lists 47 developing countries, 24 of them in Africa, which depend on agricultural exports. Many of these rely on exporting a single crop such as coffee, sugar, cotton or, in the case of Madagascar, vanilla. This can be dangerous, as Madagascar found when it was challenged by cheaper vanilla coming onto the market from Indonesia. For such countries, a bad harvest at home can wipe out a year's export earnings, while a good harvest elsewhere may flood the market.

Marco Polo opened the trade routes from Europe to China in the Middle Ages. The Silk Road existed long before and was very active in Roman times.

Many countries have set out to diversify their production. But most of the foreign exchange earned by over half of all developing countries still comes from just one or two commodities.

Since 1970, sub-Saharan Africa and Latin America and the Caribbean have all seen their share of global trade fall, while the proportion enjoyed by East and Southeast Asia has grown.

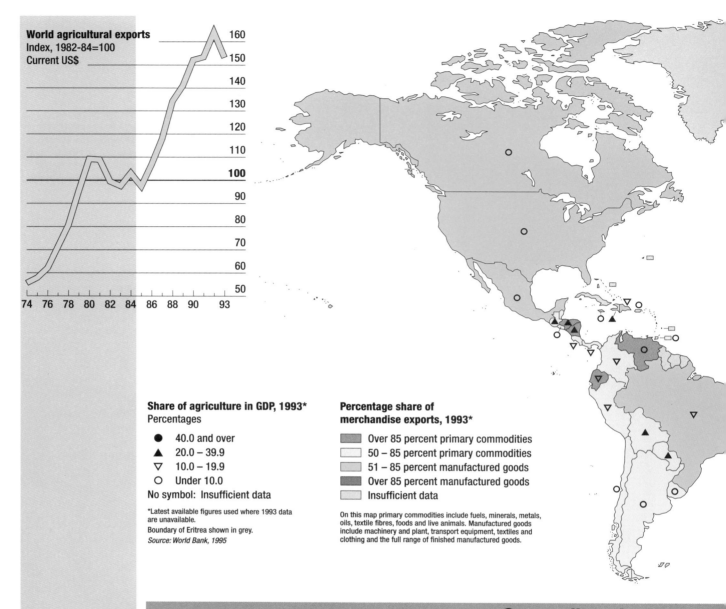

World agricultural exports
Index, 1982-84=100
Current US$

Share of agriculture in GDP, 1993*
Percentages

● 40.0 and over
▲ 20.0 – 39.9
▽ 10.0 – 19.9
○ Under 10.0
No symbol: Insufficient data

*Latest available figures used where 1993 data
are unavailable.
Boundary of Eritrea shown in grey.
Source: World Bank, 1995

**Percentage share of
merchandise exports, 1993***

Over 85 percent primary commodities
50 – 85 percent primary commodities
51 – 85 percent manufactured goods
Over 85 percent manufactured goods
Insufficient data

On this map primary commodities include fuels, minerals, metals,
oils, textile fibres, foods and live animals. Manufactured goods
include machinery and plant, transport equipment, textiles and
clothing and the full range of finished manufactured goods.

Commodity prices

Agricultural commodities are a major source of income for most developing countries other than those that have oil reserves, but prices have tended to fall over recent decades while those of manufactured goods have risen steadily. During the 1980s, recession and slow growth in the developed countries kept demand and prices low.

Between 1960 and 1987, the prices of 33 commodities monitored by the World Bank halved. The value of a 60 kilogram sack of coffee worth US$ 310 in 1977, had fallen to US$ 143 in 1989 and was worth only US$ 79 in March 1993. Between 1982 and 1992 the real cost of a kilogram of cocoa fell by about 60 percent, a kilogram of cotton by 40 percent and a kilogram of rubber by 45 percent. Although prices improved in 1994, they still stood below their 1980 level.

Meanwhile the prices of manufactured products imported by developing countries were rising – by 25 percent between 1980 and 1988. Overall, in the 1980s, the raw materials exported by developing countries lost 40 percent of their value in relation to the manufactured goods they imported.

Agricultural commodity prices are highly unstable because of fluctuations in supply and demand. Competition aggravates the situation – 62 developing countries, for example, vie for a share of the world's coffee market. Between 1972 and 1983, coffee prices fluctuated wildly each year – by an average of 36 percent above or below the trend. Furthermore, most commodities are processed after leaving their country of origin, which therefore does

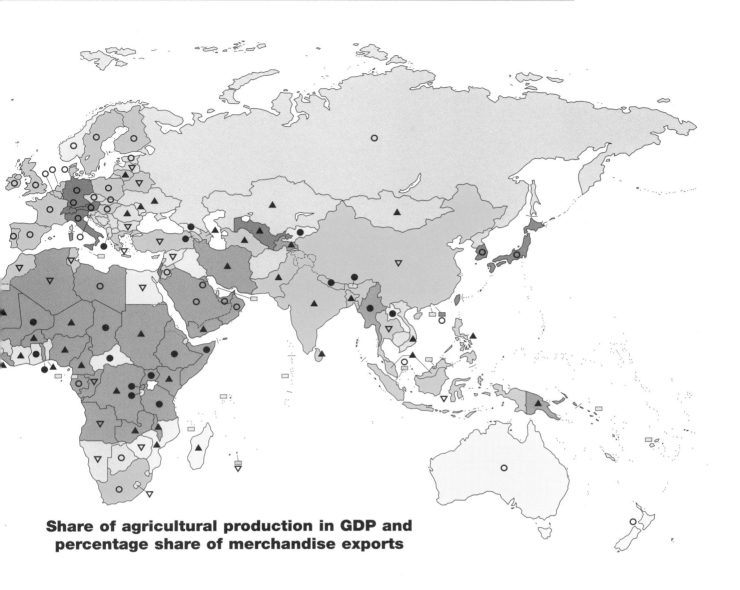

Share of agricultural production in GDP and percentage share of merchandise exports

Price indices

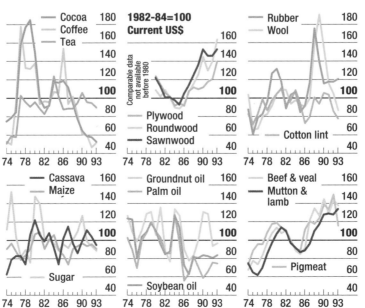

— Cocoa	180	
— Coffee	160	
— Tea	140	
	120	
	100	
	80	
	60	
	40	
74 78 82 86 90 93		

1982-84=100
Current US$

Comparable data not available before 1980

	160
	140
	120
	100
	80
— Plywood	60
— Roundwood	
— Sawnwood	40
74 78 82 86 90 93	

— Rubber	180
— Wool	160
	140
	120
	100
	80
— Cotton lint	60
	40
74 78 82 86 90 93	

— Cassava	160
— Maize	140
	120
	100
	80
— Sugar	60
	40
74 78 82 86 90 93	

— Groundnut oil	160
— Palm oil	140
	120
	100
	80
	60
— Soybean oil	40
74 78 82 86 90 93	

— Beef & veal	160
— Mutton & lamb	140
	120
	100
	80
— Pigmeat	60
	40
74 78 82 86 90 93	

not benefit from the added value that this brings. Sri Lanka keeps less than a quarter of the price of each packet of its tea that is sold in the United Kingdom – and even less reaches the farmer.

Monitoring world trade in agriculture, fisheries and forest products is one of the prime tasks for which FAO was established. FAO monitors closely policy developments in commodity markets and provides fora for discussions of emerging commodity problems through its various intergovernmental groups.

Wheat

Several major wheat producing countries do not rely on it as their main staple, but many wheat importing countries do.

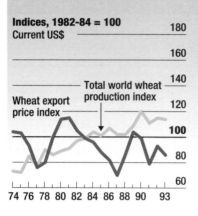

Indices, 1982-84 = 100
Current US$

180
160
140
120
100
80
60

Wheat export price index

Total world wheat production index

74 76 78 80 82 84 86 88 90 93

The cultivation of wheat dates back about 7 000 years. It originated in the western part of Asia, gradually spreading to nearly all other regions in the world. It is not surprising, therefore, that wheat, together with rice, are the two most important and common food staples in the world.

Wheat production has grown considerably over the past two decades and in recent years its global production has reached around 550 million tonnes. The total wheat output of the developing countries accounts for over 40 percent of global wheat production, with China the world's largest producer.

Wheat is the most important cereal traded on international markets. The total world trade in wheat and wheat flour (in grain equivalent) is close to 95 million tonnes, with the developing countries accounting for some 80 percent of imports. This is mainly because, despite a relatively large wheat output in the developing world, overall consumption outpaces production. As populations move from countryside to town, there is increasing demand for convenient foods such as bread. The United States ranks as the world's largest wheat exporter, normally contributing around one-third of world export volume.

Wheat is the major commodity provided as food aid. In 1992/93, for example, wheat accounted for just over half of the 15 200 tonnes of the cereal shipped as food aid to developing countries.

Rice

Rice is the staple food of almost half the world's population, but very little of the total production is traded on world markets.

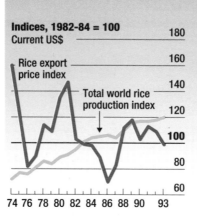

Indices, 1982-84 = 100
Current US$

180
160
140
120
100
80
60

Rice export price index

Total world rice production index

74 76 78 80 82 84 86 88 90 93

Developing countries account for about 95 percent of production and about 80 percent of trade in rice. Most of the rice, a staple food for almost half the people in the world, is consumed in the countries where it is produced. Only about 3-5 percent of rice produced is traded on the world market.

Different countries and regions have specific preferences for particular kinds of rice. Australia, the northern part of China, the Republic of Korea, Japan and Italy, for example, eat short/medium grain rice of the Japonica type. The preference in most parts of Asia and Africa is for the long grain or Indica type.

Further preferences exist within these broad categories. The varieties of Japonica rice consumed in Italy, for example, are not acceptable to consumers in Japan or the Republic of Korea.

Different countries also prefer different kinds of processing: in Bangladesh, people like parboiled rice (rice that is dehusked after being steamed); in Jordan, the preference is for camolino rice (rice treated with paraffin oil), and the Senegalese like milled white rice with a high proportion of broken grains.

Rice is one of the most difficult food commodities in which to trade because of rigid consumer preferences, the small quantities involved and the dependence of production on local climatic conditions. Fluctuations in prices on international markets can be large, adding to the uncertainties of providing this essential food.

Jute

Jute is a fibre crop which is used mainly for sacking, but efforts are being made to diversify into other end-uses. The principal producers of jute are Bangladesh, China, India, Myanmar, Nepal and Thailand. Despite the significant role played by jute in these Asian economies, the increasing use of synthetic substitutes such as plastics has made serious inroads into the global trade.

Being a natural fibre, jute is biodegradable and as such "environmentally friendly". The principal products such as sacks, can be re-used and, as a result, may have a secondary value for other users. Despite such positive features, the world market for jute has remained depressed.

In recent years, world production of jute has been about 3 million tonnes per year, of which 300 000 tonnes are traded internationally in the form of raw fibre and 900 000 tonnes in the form of products. The world trade in jute products is dominated by the following, in order of importance: sacking, yarn, hessian and carpet backing.

In the mid-1960s about 20 percent of world jute was processed in developed regions. This share has now fallen to around 5 percent. This decline results from the increased concentration of jute processing industries in the major producing and consuming countries of Asia coupled with a decline in overall consumption elsewhere because of the spread of synthetic products.

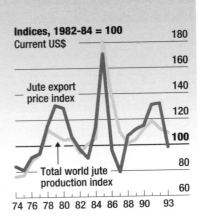

Indices, 1982-84 = 100
Current US$

Jute export price index

Total world jute production index

180 160 140 120 100 80 60

74 76 78 80 82 84 86 88 90 93

Outside of the major jute producing countries, the spread of synthetic products has reduced demand so that international trade in jute is declining.

Shrimp/shrimp products

Fish products are an important source of foreign exchange earnings in many developing countries. One success story is the trade in shrimp, a particularly high-value product.

In 1995, Thailand's harvest of the black tiger shrimp (*Penaeus monodon*), which accounts for more than one-quarter of world production of warm-water shrimps, exceeded 250 000 tonnes, confirming the country's position as the top farmed-shrimp producer. Almost half of the United States' shrimp imports consist of this species. Production of black tiger shrimps, found throughout Asia, is growing by an estimated 20 percent a year.

Trade in shrimp products has doubled in the past decade to reach 1 million tonnes but increases in aquaculture production have led to instances of market saturation, accompanied by dramatic falls in prices.

Shrimp prices also reflect fluctuations in consumption: traditionally, demand is high at Chinese New Year in Asian countries with large Chinese communities, while in Japan (the world's largest importer) demand generally slackens in February, the coldest month.

As shrimp cultivation has expanded, disease, water pollution and inadequate quality control have all had a major impact on production and trade. Thailand, China, India, Cambodia and Bangladesh have experienced severe financial losses, mainly as a result of diseased stock. The most serious decline was reported by China in 1993, when production fell from 220 000 to 35 000 tonnes. Income loss was estimated at US$ 9 770 million.

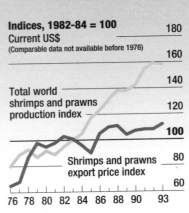

Indices, 1982-84 = 100
Current US$
(Comparable data not available before 1976)

Total world shrimps and prawns production index

Shrimps and prawns export price index

180 160 140 120 100 80 60

76 78 80 82 84 86 88 90 93

Shrimp cultivation is a growing industry in several developing countries and a major source of export earnings.

Effect of the Uruguay Round on future international food prices
Percentage change between 1987-89 and 2000

Minus value

Baseline | Uruguay Round effect | Total*

-10 0 10 20 30 40

Wheat **4**

Rice **15**

Maize **7**

Millet/sorghum **10**

Other grains **5**

Fats and oils **0**

Oil-meal proteins **3**

Bovine meat **14**

Pigmeat **13**

Sheep meat **24**

Poultry **14**

Milk **41**

*Total does not necessarily equal the sum of the two effects

The actual values shown include tariffs and other policy effects and forms of protection. The baseline is a projection for the year 2000 on the same basis. The Uruguay Round effect demonstrates how an adjustment in tariffs will increase trade.

GATT and the World Trade Organization

Policies designed to protect industry and agriculture in the developed countries make it hard for developing countries to compete in the world market. Some major developed countries sell their products at less than the cost of production, doing serious damage to non-subsidizing countries, particularly the developing country farmers.

In 1993, total support provided to agricultural producers in OECD countries amounted to US$ 163 000 million. This gives their farmers an advantage in world markets, and has led to overproduction. In 1993, one-fifth of the European Community Common Agricultural Policy budget was spent on storing its food surpluses. Producers in developed countries are also protected by tariff barriers. These tend to rise with the degree of processing involved – the tariffs for metal products and clothes, for instance, are double those for metal and cloth and four times those for metal ores and cotton. Quotas and quality controls also deter imports into their markets.

Such obstacles discourage developing countries from exporting processed agricultural products. Agricultural protectionism alone is thought to cost them US$ 100 000 million a year in lost revenues.

The General Agreement on Tariffs and Trade (GATT), signed in 1948, and the United Nations Conference on Trade and Development (UNCTAD), set up in 1964, have provided fora for negotiations on trade liberalization with some success. When GATT was established, tariffs accounted for 40 percent of the price of imported goods, on average. Today this has fallen to 5 percent.

FAO provided technical support for the latest set of GATT negotiations, the Uruguay Round, which was successfully completed in April 1994 and was the first to include agriculture significantly. As a result of the negotiations, GATT has now become the World Trade Organization (WTO), set up to monitor and regulate international trade, and to oversee the implementation of the Uruguay Round agreements. Although the reductions in subsidies and trade barriers in agriculture are small, they are expected to add over US$ 9 000 million to the value of developing countries' agricultural exports by the year 2000.

Regional trade agreements are increasingly important. The European Union (EU) has just been expanded to 15 members. The North American Free Trade Agreement (NAFTA), signed by Canada, Mexico and the United States in 1992, will abolish most trade barriers between its members and is expected to attract new members from Latin America. Other regional agreements include MERCOSUR in Latin America, CARICOM in the Caribbean, ASEAN in Asia and COMESA in Africa, among others.

Agricultural trade of developing countries

- Trade, 1987-89
- Projected trade in 2000 (baseline)
- Projected trade in 2000 (as a result of the Uruguay Round)

US$ thousand million

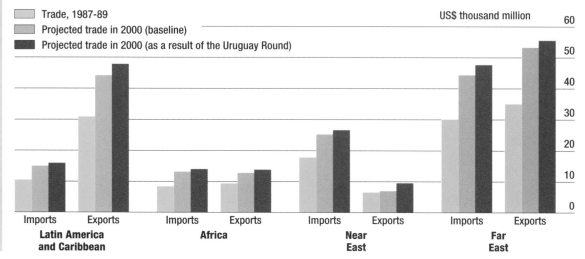

	Latin America and Caribbean	Africa	Near East	Far East
	Imports / Exports	Imports / Exports	Imports / Exports	Imports / Exports

Food aid

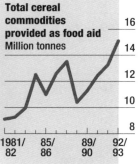

Food aid can meet immediate needs and contribute to development.

Food aid recipients
Million tonnes

Africa

Asia

Others

1981/82 — 85/86 — 89/90 — 92/93

Total cereal commodities provided as food aid
Million tonnes

1981/82 — 85/86 — 89/90 — 92/93

Total cereal imports of low-income food-deficit countries
Million tonnes

Commercial

Food aid

1981/82 — 85/86 — 89/90 — 92/93

WFP emergency operations
US$ million

Man-made disasters

Drought/crop failures

Sudden natural disasters

1982 — 85 — 88 — 91 — 93

Almost all the food reaching the poorest nations from abroad does so through trade rather than aid. Nearly 90 percent of the cereals imported by the 88 low-income food-deficit countries (LIFDCs) in the developing world and in Central and Eastern Europe in 1993 were bought on the open market.

Food aid accounts for some 5 percent of the total aid of US$ 2 600 million given by the Organisation for Economic Cooperation and Development (OECD) in 1993. Minimum food aid commitments have been established and monitored by the International Wheat Council through a series of Food Aid Conventions since 1967. Food aid may be given in kind, as a grant or on concessional terms, or in cash, to fund food imports. Triangular transactions, where the donor buys food from one developing country to give to another, help both producing and consuming nations, but only account for a small proportion of the total.

The Committee on Food Aid Policies and Programmes, elected by FAO Council and the UN's Economic and Social Council, coordinates food aid within the UN system. It is also the governing body of the World Food Programme (WFP), which is responsible for about a quarter of all food aid given every year (the rest coming directly from governments and aid agencies). Standby food aid pledges are managed by the International Emergency Food Reserve (IEFR), set up by a special session of the UN General Assembly.

Food aid may be given in response to crises caused by bad harvests, war or natural disasters (emergency food aid) or to boost development (programme or project food aid), for example, by providing food for work in support of projects for reforestation or soil conservation.

If poorly designed, food aid can create dependence in recipient countries, undercut domestic food production and nurture tastes for imported foods. But well-designed programmes and infrastructural improvements – which reach those most in need, take local eating habits into account and promote local agricultural production – can be an important tool in development.

Beating the debt burden

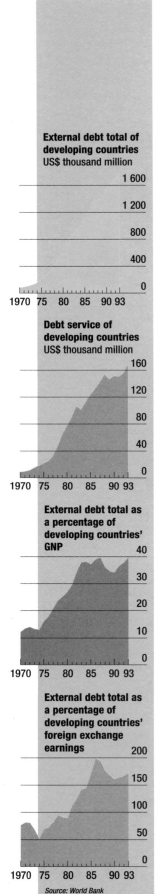

External debt total of developing countries
US$ thousand million

1 600
1 200
800
400
0

1970 75 80 85 90 93

Debt service of developing countries
US$ thousand million

160
120
80
40
0

1970 75 80 85 90 93

External debt total as a percentage of developing countries' GNP

40
30
20
10
0

1970 75 80 85 90 93

External debt total as a percentage of developing countries' foreign exchange earnings

200
150
100
50
0

1970 75 80 85 90 93

Source: World Bank

External debt total as a percentage of foreign exchange earnings

- ■ Latin America and Caribbean
- ☐ Sub-Saharan Africa
- ▨ South Asia
- ▨ East Asia and Pacific

400
350
300
250
200
150
100
50
0

1980   1987   1993

Source: World Bank

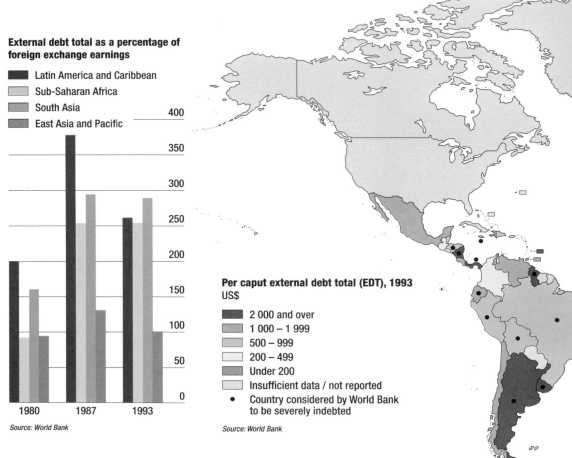

Per caput external debt total (EDT), 1993
US$

- ■ 2 000 and over
- ▨ 1 000 – 1 999
- ▨ 500 – 999
- ☐ 200 – 499
- ▨ Under 200
- ☐ Insufficient data / not reported
- • Country considered by World Bank to be severely indebted

Source: World Bank

In 1994, the developing countries as a whole owed an estimated US$ 1 800 000 million to banks, governments and multilateral institutions in the industrialized countries – the equivalent of half their entire annual trade. Servicing these huge debts diverts funds from urgently needed social and economic development.

The debt crisis dates from the oil price rises of the early 1970s. Commercial banks, flooded with money from the oil-exporting nations, found eager borrowers in developing countries. A major attraction for many of them was the low, often negative, interest rates. In theory the loans were to fund projects which would generate enough money to repay them; in practice this often failed to

happen. In April 1982, as interest rates soared, Mexico said that it could no longer pay even the interest on its debt. Other countries followed.

As the crisis grew in the 1980s, debtor nations turned to the IMF and World Bank for help. These institutions made their help conditional on stringent structural adjustment programmes, which often included devaluation and cuts in public spending. These hit the poorest hardest.

The world's largest debtor is the United States, but because of its developed economy and rich resources, it has little problem servicing its debt and continuing to attract investment. Developing countries are far less well placed, spending about

one-fifth of all their export earnings for debt servicing. In 1994 the debt of sub-Saharan Africa (excluding South Africa) was 10 percent higher than its annual output. Every year the region spends four times more on servicing its debt than it does on health and education combined. Central and Eastern European countries face similar dilemmas.

Over the past ten years, about 80 percent of the debts owed by the developing countries to commercial banks have been renegotiated on more favourable terms. This restructuring and rescheduling (lowering debt service costs by spreading the debt over a longer period of time) has eased the burden of the most indebted continent, Latin

Many developing countries are so indebted that their total annual repayments outstrip foreign exchange earnings up to 30 times over.

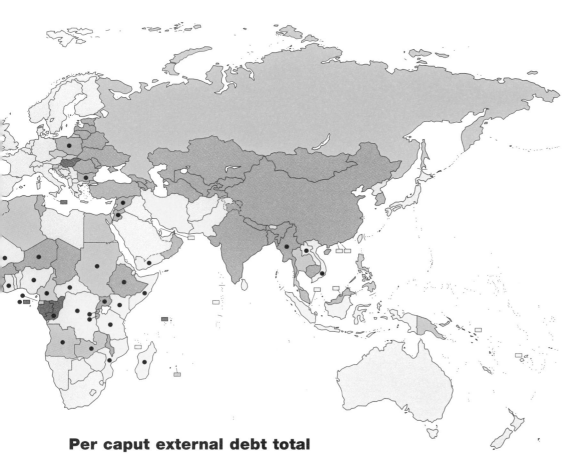

Per caput external debt total

America. Some countries have had part of their debt forgiven.

Debt swaps – by which foreign investors write off part of a country's debt in exchange for local currency which they invest within the debtor nation – provide another mechanism. A refinement – debt-for-nature swaps – allows international environmental groups to buy part of a developing country's debt in exchange for government investment in conservation: half of Madagascar's US$ 100 million commercial bank debt has been written off in this way. But with a value by 1995 of less than US$ 750 million, these are unlikely to relieve much of the developing world's debt burden.

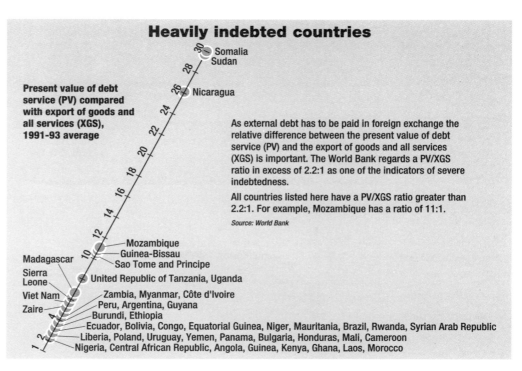

Heavily indebted countries

Present value of debt service (PV) compared with export of goods and all services (XGS), 1991-93 average

As external debt has to be paid in foreign exchange the relative difference between the present value of debt service (PV) and the export of goods and all services (XGS) is important. The World Bank regards a PV/XGS ratio in excess of 2.2:1 as one of the indicators of severe indebtedness.

All countries listed here have a PV/XGS ratio greater than 2.2:1. For example, Mozambique has a ratio of 11:1.

Source: World Bank

- 30 — Somalia
- Sudan
- 26 — Nicaragua
- Mozambique
- Guinea-Bissau
- Sao Tome and Principe
- Madagascar
- United Republic of Tanzania, Uganda
- Sierra Leone
- Zambia, Myanmar, Côte d'Ivoire
- Viet Nam — Peru, Argentina, Guyana
- Zaire — Burundi, Ethiopia
- Ecuador, Bolivia, Congo, Equatorial Guinea, Niger, Mauritania, Brazil, Rwanda, Syrian Arab Republic
- Liberia, Poland, Uruguay, Yemen, Panama, Bulgaria, Honduras, Mali, Cameroon
- Nigeria, Central African Republic, Angola, Guinea, Kenya, Ghana, Laos, Morocco

The challenge of food production

Between 1950 and 1980 food production in developing countries grew at an average of 3 percent a year, a rate that exceeded that of population growth. This unparalleled increase, largely due to the adoption of new high-yielding varieties, bought time for the development of further solutions to world food problems.

Until the second half of this century, agricultural research focused largely on the needs of industrialized countries; where it reached the developing countries, it was directed for the most part towards crops that were important to the developed world. After the Second World War – and particularly after the food crisis of the 1960s – the focus began to change. International research centres were founded and local scientists trained. Sub-Saharan Africa now has four times more scientists than it did in 1961, although expenditure on research has fallen.

Research in Mexico and the Philippines in the 1950s and 1960s led to the development of the high-yielding varieties of wheat and rice that launched the Green Revolution. Between 1950 and 1980, production of food in the developing world rose by an average of 3 percent a year, outstripping

population growth. India's wheat production trebled between 1967 and 1982; rice production in the Philippines doubled between 1960 and 1980. Today, high-yielding varieties cover half the world's wheatlands and most of its rice paddies. The extra rice produced, alone, feeds 700 million people.

The success of the first high-yielding varieties depended on the availability of water, chemical fertilizers and pesticides and on the use of machinery – favouring prosperous farmers and those with access to water and transport. The revolution was mostly confined to Asia and parts of Latin America, but Africa was hardly touched.

Agricultural resources

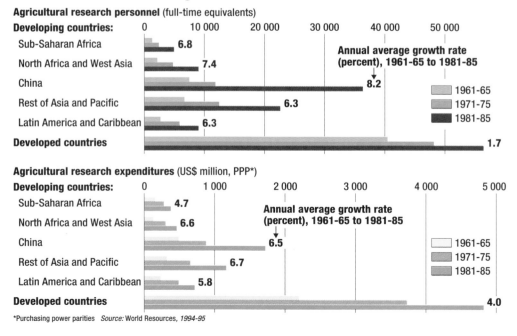

Agricultural research personnel (full-time equivalents)

Developing countries:
- Sub-Saharan Africa: 6.8
- North Africa and West Asia: 7.4
- China: 8.2
- Rest of Asia and Pacific: 6.3
- Latin America and Caribbean: 6.3
- **Developed countries**: 1.7

Annual average growth rate (percent), 1961-65 to 1981-85

Legend: 1961-65, 1971-75, 1981-85

Agricultural research expenditures (US$ million, PPP*)

Developing countries:
- Sub-Saharan Africa: 4.7
- North Africa and West Asia: 6.6
- China: 6.5
- Rest of Asia and Pacific: 6.7
- Latin America and Caribbean: 5.8
- **Developed countries**: 4.0

Annual average growth rate (percent), 1961-65 to 1981-85

Legend: 1961-65, 1971-75, 1981-85

*Purchasing power parities Source: World Resources, 1994-95

Future food security depends on high-yielding varieties of staple foods.

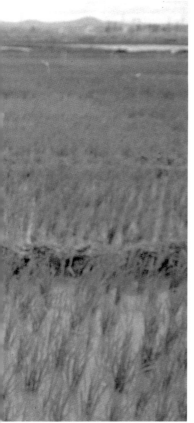

New high-yielding varieties of staple crops (rice, main picture, and barley, above) can help to provide food security for increasing populations.

There is now a new concentration on development of crops to suit less favourable soils and climates: new varieties of wheat which will grow in drought-prone climates are being developed as are strains of rice suited to the acid soils of Latin America's savannahs and the poor lowland soils of South and Southeast Asia. A hybrid rice developed in China has raised hopes of a new miracle rice which will help to boost harvests by the 74 percent that will be needed by 2020. Such breakthroughs are urgently needed: rice yields in Asia seem to have levelled out even though the population continues to increase.

Meanwhile other international research centres, set up in the 1960s and 1970s, have focused on other crops. Recent successes include new strains of faba bean – the "poor man's food" – which have transformed Egypt from an importer to an exporter of the crop; a sweet sorghum, developed in China, which is used as animal feed and for the production of alcohol for fuel; high-yielding varieties of cassava – Africa's most widely grown staple food – which doubled yields in the 1980s and are set to do so again; and a hybrid pigeon pea which offers the hope of a "green revolution" in pulses. Research has also improved methods of growing crops, such as the discovery of ways of applying fertilizer more efficiently to Chinese cabbage crops.

In all this, scientists are increasingly aware that progress depends on listening to the farmers and drawing on their own knowledge and experience.

As each new variety usually lasted for only three to four years before adaptation of pests and diseases caused its resistance to break down, scientists had to keep breeding new strains. Over 1 000 new varieties of rice have been launched since 1966.

Changing focus of agricultural research and development

Past focus	Recent additional emphasis
CROPS	
Non-food and cash crops	Upgrading subsistence food crops
Large-scale producers	Small-scale producers
Prime land	Marginal land
Increased productivity	Sustainable production
Higher-yielding cultivars	Stress-tolerant cultivars
Mechanization	Animal traction
Monocultures	Intercropping
Irrigation	Rain-fed agriculture
Mineral fertilizers	Nutrient recycling
Chemical pesticides	Integrated pest management
Limited number of crops	Crop diversification
LIVESTOCK	
Cattle	Small ruminants and other small livestock/poultry species
Large-scale producers	Small-scale producers
Traditional pastures	Improved dryland pastures
Capital-intensive production	Extensive production
	Improved feed quantity and quality
FISH	
Commercial off-shore fisheries	In-shore, inland artisanal fisheries, aquaculture
	Replenishment of stock
Increased production	Increased fishing efficiency
	Reduced post-harvest losses
	Improved monitoring of stocks
	Enhancement of marine environment
Development of boats and gear	Alternative energy propulsion
	Small-scale fishing technologies
TREES	
Single species plantations	Multipurpose tree crops
Industrial forestry	Community forestry/agroforestry
	Women in forestry
	Non-timber forest products
	Trees for watershed management
	Trees for environmental improvement
	Management of protected areas

Areas of genetic diversity of cultivated pl

- CGIAR centres
- Areas of genetic diversity of cultivated plants

CIAT International Centre of Tropical Agriculture, Cali, Colombia
- Founded 1967
- Conducts research in germplasm development in beans, cassava, tropical forages and rice for Latin America, and in resource management of humid agro-ecosystems in tropical America

CIFOR Centre for International Forestry Research, Jakarta, Indonesia
- Founded 1993
- Undertakes research in forest systems and forestry and promotes the adoption of improved technologies and management practices, to increase well-being in developing countries, particularly the tropics

CIMMYT International Centre for Improvement of Wheat and Maize, Lisboa, Mexico

- Founded 1966
- Focuses on increasing the productivity of resources committed to wheat and maize through agricultural research and in partnership with national research systems

CIP International Potato Centre, Lima, Peru
- Founded 1970
- Undertakes coordinated, multidisciplinary research programmes on potato and sweet potato and worldwide collaborative research and training

ICARDA International Centre for Agricultural Research in the Dry Areas, Aleppo, Syria
- Founded 1975
- Works towards increased and sustainable productivity of winter

rain-fed agricultural systems in a harsh and variable environment; addressing issues such as soil degradation and water use efficiency

ICLARM International Centre for Living Aquatic Resources Management, Manila, Philippines
- Founded 1977
- Aims to improve the production and management of aquatic resources of low-income users in developing countries through international research and related activities

ICRAF International Centre for Research in Agroforestry, Nairobi, Kenya
- Founded 1977
- Focuses on mitigating tropical deforestation, land depletion and rural poverty through improved agroforestry systems

Improved varieties of cereals

Research and development has produced hardier plants with shorter growing times: barley (right); wheat (far right, top); rice (far right, bottom).

CGIAR research centres

ICRISAT International Crops Research Institute for the Semi-Arid Tropics, Andhra Pradesh, India
● Founded 1972
● Conducts research into crops such as sorghum, finger millet, pearl millet, chick-pea and groundnut for enhanced sustainable food production in the harsh conditions of the semi-arid tropics

IFPRI International Food Policy Research Institute, Washington, D.C., United States
● Founded 1975
● Identifies and analyses policies for the food needs of developing countries, particularly the poorest groups. Issues addressed include food production and consumption, land use, trade and macro-economic conditions

IIMI International Irrigation Management Institute, Colombo, Sri Lanka
● Founded 1984
● Aims to strengthen the development, dissemination and adoption of lasting improvements in irrigated agriculture in developing countries

IITA International Institute of Tropical Agriculture, Ibadan, Nigeria
● Founded 1967
● Conducts research and outreach activities on crops such as maize, cassava, plantain, soybean and yam, for sustainable, increased food production in the humid and sub-humid tropics

ILRI International Livestock Research Institute, Nairobi, Kenya
● Founded 1995
● Incorporates some programmes from the former International Livestock Centre for Africa and the International

Laboratory for Research on Animal Diseases. Has global responsibilities for strategic livestock research in genetics, physiology, nutrition and health

IPGRI International Plant Genetic Resources Institute (successor to the International Board for Plant Genetic Resources, IBPGR), Rome, Italy
● Founded 1974
● Strengthens the conservation and use of plant genetic resources worldwide, with particular emphasis on developing countries, by research, training and information activities

IRRI International Rice Research Institute, Manila, Philippines
● Founded 1960
● Generates and spreads rice-related knowledge and technology of environmental, social and economic benefit and helps enhance national rice research

ISNAR International Service for National Agricultural Research, The Hague, Netherlands
● Founded 1979
● Helps developing countries bring about sustained improvements in the performance of their national agricultural research systems and organizations

WARDA West Africa Rice Development Association, Bouaké, Côte d'Ivoire
● Founded 1970
● Conducts and promotes wide-ranging rice research to improve the technical and economic options available to smallholder farm families in the Sahel, upland swamp areas and mangrove swamp environments

The agricultural research network

The Consultative Group on International Agricultural Research (CGIAR) was set up in 1971. It coordinates a global network of 16 international centres – 13 of them in the developing world – and national centres. It promotes research on food production and natural resources management and mobilizes donor support.

The CGIAR centres both develop new crop varieties and conserve the genetic resources which provide the raw material for research. They are situated in, or near, most of the richest regions of biological diversity where crops originated in the wild. They house the world's

largest *ex situ* collections of plant genetic resources: the International Rice Research Institute (IRRI) in the Philippines, for instance, conserves over 86 000 rice varieties and wild species.

Such collections play an important part in protecting food supplies: a Turkish variety of wheat, collected in 1948 and ignored for many years, has recently been found to carry genes resistant to a whole array of diseases which threaten modern crops.

When war disrupts agriculture and farmers must eat their seeds to survive, indigenous varieties can disappear. In 1986 the IRRI reintroduced rice strains to

Cambodia which had been lost during the civil war, while the CGIAR Seeds of Hope programme is replicating seeds in a bid to restore Rwanda's agriculture and genetic diversity.

CGIAR's best known work remains the development of new varieties of crops. It is breeding strains suited to poor farmers, who cannot afford heavy chemical inputs, and which will tolerate harsh conditions. Some centres concentrate on particular crop species, while the International Livestock Research Institute in Nairobi, Kenya, focuses on farm animals. Other centres are devoted to fisheries, forestry, food policy, irrigation and dryland management.

Farmers in Rwanda normally keep seed from one harvest to plant in the following season. Civil war disrupted this routine and by autumn 1994 some 850 000 families needed seed. FAO coordinated a US$ 18.4 million programme that distributed bean, maize and other seed to help restore Rwandan agriculture.

Biotechnology

Gene banks ranked by size of collection
(excludes CGIAR centres)

This gene bank in Ethiopia stores seeds of hundreds of wild varieties of crops at sub-zero temperatures for up to 50 years. Every five years the collection is tested for germination ability.

MALTA

23c

JUM DINJI DWAR L-IKEL 1981

Crops need new protection every 15 years because pests and diseases develop around their existing defences. The only effective way to confer it is to interbreed them with other strains, often wild ones.

Biotechnology can be defined as the use of living organisms to make or modify products, to improve plants or animals, or to develop micro-organisms for specific uses. It has been used since people first added yeast to bread or saved the seed from the pick of their crops for next year's sowing.

Advances in molecular biology have transformed biotechnology in recent years. Whereas in the past, crop improvement depended on selective breeding within species, developments in genetic engineering now make it possible to introduce genes from one species to another, producing "transgenic" varieties. Tissue culture, through which plants can be cloned from a single cell, has speeded up the process of making new varieties available.

The first successful experiment in gene manipulation took place in 1986. By 1990, some US$ 11 000 million a year was being spent on research and development – two-thirds of it by companies in the private sector. That year, the biotechnology industry in the United States produced some US$ 2 000 million worth of products.

So far research has concentrated on medicine and pharmacy, but the potential for agriculture is immense. By the mid-1990s, some 50 plant species had been biotechnically altered – including rice, wheat, potato, soybean and alfalfa. Resistance to pests can be bred in this way, cutting the farmer's dependence on chemicals. Scientists are also using gene manipulation to produce quicker-growing

fish and cheaper, more effective vaccines against livestock diseases. Tissue culture has been used to boost the productivity of oil palm and eucalyptus plantations.

Biotechnology has tended to favour the industrialized world, where most of the research is concentrated. Facilities are being set up in most developing countries, but progress is hindered by a lack of money and trained people. Even though these countries provide much of the genetic raw material used, their access to biotechnology is blocked by patents and other measures taken by companies in the developed world to protect their investment in research and development.

Developing countries are concerned that substances synthesized in the laboratory or produced by transgenic crops may undercut such traditional exports as vanilla, pyrethrum, rubber and coconut oil. Biotechnology may also present environmental risks. Cloned varieties could erode genetic diversity. Genes from transgenic crops could spread to wild relatives. As yet no satisfactory international standards exist for biosafety or the patenting of living organisms and genetic materials. There are plans, however, to add a biotechnology protocol to the United Nations Convention on Biological Diversity, which was agreed following the 1992 UN Conference on Environment and Development (UNCED) – generally referred to as the Earth Summit – in Rio de Janeiro.

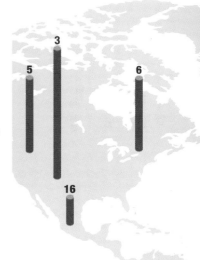

9 National Research Centre of Genetic Resources and Biotechnology, Brasilia, Brazil

10 Institute of Crop Sciences, Braunschweig, Germany

11 Plant Breeding and Acclimatization Institute, Radzikow, Poland

12 Plant Genetic Resources Centre, Addis Ababa, Ethiopia

The world's major national plant gene banks

1 Institute of Crop Germplasm Resources, Beijing, China

2 N.I. Vavilov Research Institute of Plant Industry, St Petersburg, Russian Federation

3 National Seed Storage Laboratory, Colorado, United States

4 National Bureau of Plant Genetic Resources, New Delhi, India

5 National Small Grain Collection, Idaho, United States

6 Plant Gene Resources of Canada, Ottawa, Canada

7 Institute of Plant Genetics and Crop Research, Gatersleben, Germany

8 Department of Horticulture and Fruit Breeding, University of Agricultural Science, Kristianstad, Sweden

Careful maintenance of the earth's genetic resources is vital. Genes provide the raw materials for development of new pharmaceutical, agricultural and industrial products through biotechnology.

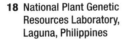

13 Institute of Germplasm, Bari, Italy

14 Institute for Agrobotany, Tapioszele, Hungary

15 Department of Genetic Resources, National Institute of Agrobiological Resources, Tsukuba, Japan

16 National Institute for Forestry and Agricultural Research, San Rafael, Mexico

17 John Innes Centre, Norwich, United Kingdom

18 National Plant Genetic Resources Laboratory, Laguna, Philippines

19 Institute of Agroecology and Biotechnology, Kiev, Ukraine

20 Australian Winter Cereals Collection, Tamworth, Australia

Biotechnology has already developed:

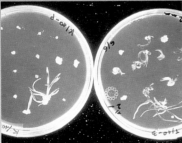

Potato plants resistant to disease: to promote growth and decrease risk of epidemics (far left).
Barley with accelerated growth rates: to increase agricultural production (top, middle left).
Onions that are slower to rot or sprout after cropping: to increase the shelf-life and reduce losses in quantity and quality (bottom, middle left).

Perennial maize
In Mexico in the late 1970s two wild ancestors of maize were found that have been called the botanical find of the century. They can confer resistance to seven of the domestic crop's major diseases and can turn it into a perennial crop, allowing it to be harvested every year without resowing (left).

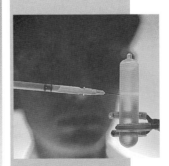

Modern biotechnology is based on genetic engineering, by which the DNA in the nucleus of cells can be modified to produce new varieties.

Self-cloning seeds

Some 300 species of plants reproduce asexually. Scientists are working on transferring this "apomixis" to crops. Seed resulting from normal reproduction combines genes from both parents and so grows into a plant with its own unique genetic make-up; but seed from an apomictic plant produces an exact genetic replica of its parent. So new varieties, designed for specific environments, could be produced much more quickly than before, and farmers would be able to gather their own seed. Apomictic maize is expected in 1997, but it could be ten years before the first crops reach the fields. Some seed companies view apomictic crops as a threat to their sales, while some environmentalists fear their possible effect on genetic diversity.

Vine-fr

The Flavr Savr tomato, the first bio-engineered food to reach the world's markets, went on sale in the United States in 1994. Biotechnologists have given the tomato an extra gene, which prevents it softening soon after it is ripe. The main benefit, according to them, is in the improved taste. Traditional tomatoes have to be picked while they are still green to prevent them rotting

Biotechnology protects biodiversity by assisting conservation of plant and animal genetic resources through:

● new methods for collecting and sorting genetic material

● detection and elimination of disease in gene bank collections

● identification of useful genes

● improved techniques for long-term storage

● safer and more efficient distribution of germplasm to users.

New crop varieties can be developed more quickly through genetic engineering than through the traditional method of cross-pollination.

A weapon against cattle plague

Most of the agricultural applications of biotechnology to date have related to animal production and health. Genetically-engineered vaccines offer a weapon against such scourges as rinderpest, which killed 2 million cattle in Africa in the early 1980s and caused indirect losses to national economies of some US$ 1 000 million. Such diseases force herders to run resistant, but low-yielding, breeds. If they could be eradicated, it would be possible to crossbreed with high-yielding European breeds and so improve production. An Ethiopian scientist, working in the United States, has now developed a genetically-engineered vaccine against rinderpest, which uses a virus to confer immunity. Unlike the previous vaccine, the new vaccine is unaffected by heat, inexpensive, virtually indestructible and produces antibodies that can easily be distinguished from those produced by the disease – a characteristic useful for monitoring protection against infection. Tailored genetically engineered vaccines also exist for other livestock diseases, including pig scours and chicken bursal disease.

Nitrog

Rice needs 1 kilogram of nitrogen to produce 15-20 kilograms of grain, but only takes up one-third to one-half of any chemical fertilizer applied. Leguminous plants such as peas and beans produce their own fertilizer, through the rhizobia bacteria in their root nodules, which fix nitrogen from the atmosphere. Biotechnologists are working on transferring

...matoes

before they reach the customer. The new variety, however, can be left to ripen on the vine and because of this it retains its "homegrown" taste. The Flavr Savr tomato is the first food to benefit from the United States Government's ruling, in 1992, which stated that food derived from gene-altered plants is not required to undergo any special tests.

A tool for conservation

Biotechnology offers scientists new methods for conserving genetic diversity, particularly useful for plants which are sterile or have poor germination rates and whose seeds do not store well. Tissue culture makes it possible to store cells, as opposed to seeds or plants. Cryopreservation – storage at very low temperatures – freezes cell development and has been used successfully for cassava, coffee, banana and sugar cane germplasm. These methods require less space than preserving cuttings *in vitro* or in field collections, which are vulnerable to pests, disease and disasters. Biotechnology also makes it possible to detect and eliminate diseases in gene bank collections and offers more efficient ways of distributing germplasm to users.

Biotechnology in the developing world is hampered by:

● inadequate funding/ lack of human resources

● restricted information

● poor higher education

● weak links between universities and research institutions

● lack of appropriate legal regimes

● little private sector involvement.

However, many countries in the developing world have considerable potential for biotechnology because of their wealth of biodiversity.

...ng rice

this characteristic to rice plants, either by turning them into legumes or encouraging nitrogen-fixing bacteria in the soil to move into their root cells. This could save poor farmers large sums of money, and transform yields in such regions as Southeast Asia, where an area larger than Sweden and Norway has soils too poor to sustain high-yielding rice varieties.

Eradicating the screwworm

The New World screwworm fly's scientific name, *Cochliomyia hominivorax*, describes its ability to "devour humans", but its main menace is to livestock. It lays up to 400 eggs in the open wounds of warm-blooded creatures, including people: the maggots then eat into the living flesh. It used to cause losses in the United States alone of over US$ 100 million a year.

The New World screwworm has now been eradicated from the United States and Mexico using biotechnology. The larvae of the flies are sterilized. When mature, ten sterile males are released for every unsterilized one thought to be in the area: they mate with females which produce no offspring. As a result the population is gradually reduced. The last screwworm case in the United States was reported in 1982, the last in Mexico in 1990.

In 1989 the pest spread, probably carried by imported animals, to Africa when there was an outbreak in the Libyan Arab Jamahiriya. FAO organized a campaign flying sterile insects from a "fly factory" in Mexico. Within two years the fly had been successfully eradicated using this sterile insect technique (SIT) and a potential disaster had been avoided.

The view from space: Building models of the world

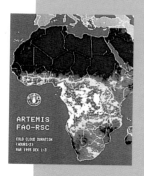

ARTEMIS draws upon satellite data to forecast crop production as well as conditions that might favour the buildup of locusts.

Remote sensing involves the collection and interpretation of information about something with which the sensor has no physical contact. Once simply a matter of climbing a hill and observing the lay of the land, it has evolved through black-and-white aerial photography into a complex process, using imaging radar, thermal scanning and satellites.

Modern remote sensing is based on picking up the electromagnetic energy emitted or reflected into space by different features on the earth's surface. This can provide information on geological structures, surface water, land use, soil conditions, vegetation, the oceans and a wide range of other factors relevant to agricultural and natural resource planning.

FAO's comprehensive assessment of the world's forest resources, published in 1995, drew upon remote sensing data and other national statistics. The Organization is now working on a land cover database for Africa. Such activities form part of the Global Environment Monitoring System (GEMS), a worldwide collective effort coordinated by the United Nations Environment Programme.

Two kinds of satellites are used for studying natural resources. Earth resources satellites, such as the United States' Landsat, France's SPOT and Japan's MOS, provide the detailed resolution (between 10 and 80 metres) required for thematic mapping of such things as land cover or erosion. FAO has drawn on data from earth resources

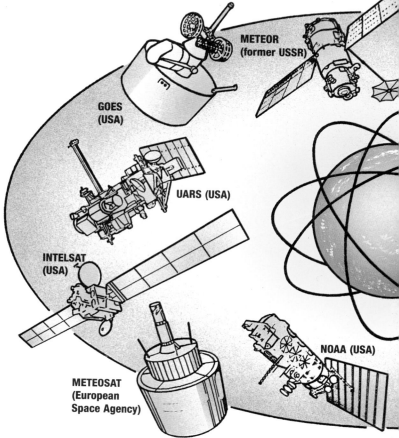

satellites for thematic mapping projects in over 70 countries.

Environmental satellites, such as Europe's Meteosat or the United States' NOAA and AVHRR, offer more frequent but less detailed pictures of areas as large as countries or continents. FAO has used them to monitor rainfall and vegetation in Africa and the Near East. This information is processed by the computer system ARTEMIS (the Africa Real Time Environmental Monitoring Information System) and used to predict harvests, drought, locust swarms and food aid requirements.

Information from ARTEMIS is used by FAO's Global Information and Early

Warning System (GIEWS) and its Desert Locust Plague Prevention Group.

Remote sensing satellites, 900 kilometres up in space, enable scientists to monitor the conditions for crop production or which might encourage desert locusts to breed in large numbers. Since 1992 early warning of food crises and natural disasters has been transmitted to regional processing centres in Kenya, Ghana and Zimbabwe via the satellite telecommunications system DIANA (the Direct Information Access Network for Africa).

OLIVIA, a satellite environmental monitoring programme for Asia and the Pacific, is currently being developed.

The new technologies of remote sensing and Geographic Information Systems (GIS) make it possible to gather, integrate and analyse vast bodies of data that can then be used to tackle complex environmental problems.

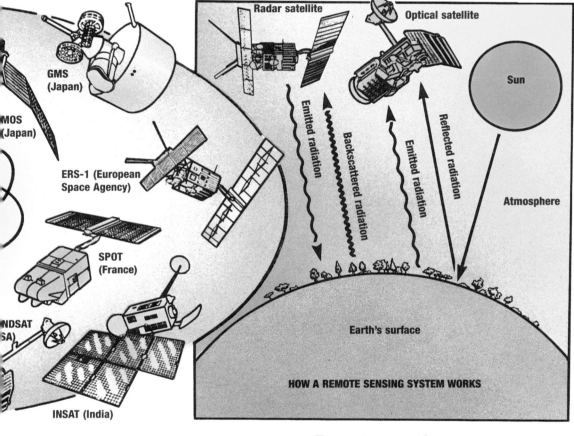

GMS (Japan)

MOS (Japan)

ERS-1 (European Space Agency)

SPOT (France)

LANDSAT (USA)

INSAT (India)

Radar satellite

Optical satellite

Sun

Emitted radiation

Backscattered radiation

Emitted radiation

Reflected radiation

Atmosphere

Earth's surface

HOW A REMOTE SENSING SYSTEM WORKS

Remote sensing

Remote sensors record and monitor the earth's surface by measuring the various emissions or reflections of electromagnetic energy from different types of vegetation, soils and other features.

This data is then colour coded to produce an image (left). Here red represents forest, blue/green, agricultural land, and purple, rocky outcrops

The image is then verified by ground sampling (far left): olive groves (top), high land (middle), pasture (bottom).

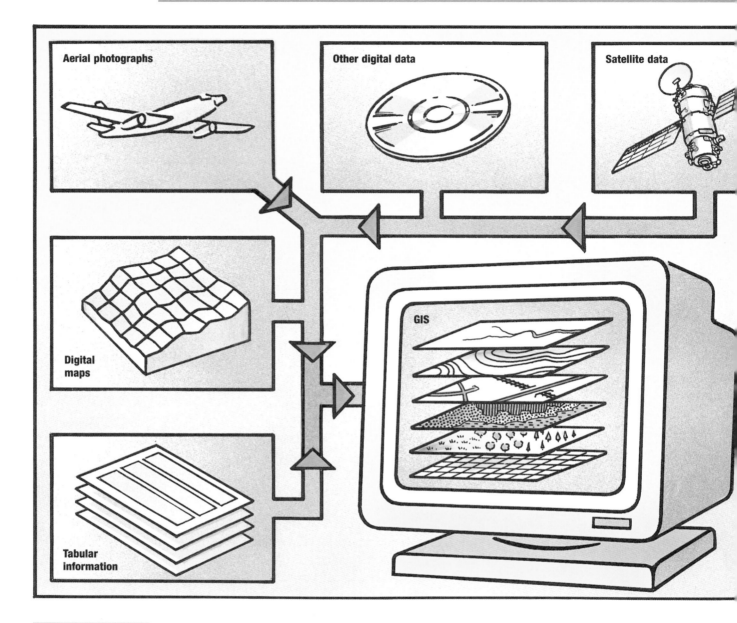

Aerial photographs

Other digital data

Satellite data

Digital maps

GIS

Tabular information

Resource use planning depends on correlating a vast quantity of data. For instance, a planner trying to locate suitable sites for growing a particular crop must combine information about soils, topography, rainfall, land tenure, transport, infrastructure, labour availability and distance from markets. This involves reconciling maps of different scales and types with tables of statistics and written information.

Until the early 1980s, this was a laborious process, achieved by overlaying transparent maps on light tables. Such manual integration of different soil maps used to prepare FAO's Soil Map of the World, for instance, took an estimated 150 person-years of work.

Introduction of the Geographic Information System (GIS) has transformed the situation. Once the data, often derived from remote sensing, have been entered into the computer system, they can be combined with other data to provide a wide range of outputs, including three-dimensional views, maps and tables. It is even possible to animate events. GIS can also be used to model the effect of a specific process over a period of time for a particular scenario.

FAO is harnessing GIS to help planners in the developing world make a wide range of decisions. It has been used, for example, to identify areas in Africa with potential for different kinds of irrigation, to assess the suitability of land for forestry and to map Kenya's agro-ecological zones. GIS helped Costa Rica to pinpoint the best sites for aquaculture in the Gulf of Nicoya.

GIS can also be a tool for the conservation of genetic resources. When the characteristics of places where samples have been found in the past are merged with maps of unexplored areas, GIS can give collectors an idea of new

A GIS integrates various types and styles of data which have been collected using a number of different systems. For example, a user could overlay data about climate, crops and population to establish optimum use of agricultural land for food production.

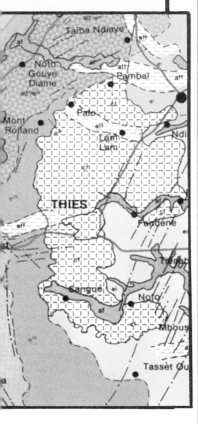

Tsetse fly in Africa

Ford and Katondo tsetse distribution map

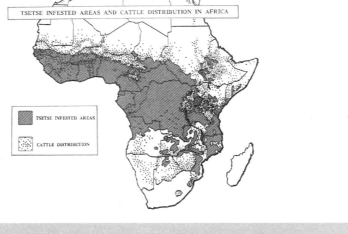

palpalis group

Idrisi

TSETSE INFESTED AREAS AND CATTLE DISTRIBUTION IN AFRICA

TSETSE INFESTED AREAS

CATTLE DISTRIBUTION

Two of many electronic maps produced by FAO using GIS for environmental management and planning.

locations to search for germplasm. It can also provide an inventory of the species, characteristics and environmental conditions of a given area as an aid to *in situ* conservation.

In 1987, the former International Laboratory for Research on Animal Diseases used GRID, a GIS developed by UNEP, to investigate the environmental factors which limit the range of East Coast Fever, a tick-borne disease which kills many cattle in Africa. Data on climate, vegetation and cattle range were combined to identify high-risk areas where the disease might spread if infected cattle were introduced.

GIS data on the current incidence and distribution of tsetse fly in Africa are used to assess, among other things, where cattle can be safely kept or where they might require protection.

The top map shows the present distribution of the palpalis group. This is a riverine species of tsetse fly which congregates in humid and sub-humid zones.

The bottom map shows cattle distribution superimposed on tsetse infested areas, thus giving an approximate picture of the current encroachment of the tsetse fly on grazing areas. It suggests that around

10 percent of the subcontinent's cattle are being kept within the tsetse-infested area. The dots on the periphery of the red area represent cattle distribution in the tsetse-free drylands.

GIS is used to identify high-risk areas that are then targeted in cattle vaccination programmes.

Transfer of technology

Some technology transfer opportunities:

LAND/WATER
• assessment of agro-ecological potential
• sustainable resource management
• improved water management technologies

CROPS/LIVESTOCK
• seed/fertilizer production and distribution
• integrated pest management (IPM)
• re-evaluation of traditional crops
• use of animal power
• dairy cooperatives
• animal breed improvement
• pest/disease control
• food processing
• post-harvest loss prevention

FISHERIES
• resource surveys
• aquaculture
• fish processing and marketing

FORESTRY
• community forestry and agroforestry
• policy development
• nurseries and plantations
• forest industries

RURAL DEVELOPMENT
• people's participation
• access to markets and credit
• agricultural training
• appropriate technology to assist rural women
• rural energy

FOOD SECURITY AND NUTRITION
• quality control
• early warning systems
• remote sensing
• food stock management and distribution

Major FAO information systems
• AGRIS (International Information System for the Agricultural Sciences and Technology)
• ARTEMIS (Remote Sensing Database)
• ASFIS (Aquatic Sciences and Fisheries Information System)
• CARIS (Current Agricultural Research Information System)
• FAOSTAT (Statistical Database for WAICENT)
• FISHDAB (Fisheries Statistical Database)
• FIPIS (Fishery Project Information System)
• FORIS (Forest Resources Information System)
• GDAGR (Global Databank for Animal Genetic Resources)
• GIEWS (Global Information and Early Warning System)
• GIS (Geographic Information System)
• GIS-DAD (Global Information System for Domestic Animal Diversity)
• GLOBEFISH (International Fish Market Indicators)
• Land Resource Data Bank
• Plant Nutrition Data Bank
• Seed Information System
• WAICENT (World Agricultural Information Centre)
• WIEWS (World Information and Early Warning System on Plant Genetic Resources)
• World Forest Resources Inventory

Regional centres and organizations provide technical inputs, research, training, and disseminate information to promote regional cooperation. They include:
• CARDNE (Centre for Agrarian Reform and Rural Development in the Near East)
• CIRDAFRICA (Centre for Integrated Rural Development in Africa)
• CIRDAP (Centre on Integrated and Rural Development for Asia and the Pacific)
• SADC (Southern African Development Community)

Regional networks/programmes coordinate research, information and technical cooperation. They include:
• Coordination of Rinderpest Eradication in West Africa project (including cattle vaccination) – 11 countries
• Latin American Technical Cooperation Network on Watershed Management – 20 countries
• Near East Regional Research and Development Network on Small Ruminants – 10 countries
• Pacific Island countries cooperation in root crop production and development – 12 countries
• Regional Cooperative Programme for Improvement of Food Legumes and Coarse Grains – 14 Asian countries
• Regional Cooperative Research Programme (Network) on Fish Technology in Africa – 16 countries

St Lucia
To Jamaica:
• assistance in sea moss development

Trinidad and To[b]
Development and pr[o]
projects:
• rural energy techn[o]
solar dryers

Costa Rica
Development and promotion projects:
• wood gasification for rural energy

Ecuador
To Dominican Republic:
• banana quality and marketing improvements

Peru
Development and promotion projects:
• small-scale hydropower (also Colombia and Bolivia)

Brazil
To other Latin American countries:
• tropical forest management techniques
Development and promotion projects:
• wood gasification for rural energy
• small-scale hydropower

Argentina
Exchanges:
• trained Ch[i]
technician[s]
biotechnol[ogy]
• helped Nig[eria]
oilseed an[d]
research programm[e]

Exchange of ideas, skills and techniques is vital if the majority of the world's people are to benefit from technological advances. There is nothing new about this: the Babylonians taught the ancient world how to make bricks. Since the colonial era, technology transfer has tended to be a matter of patronage between developed and developing countries, rather than an equal exchange. While this type of cooperation continues to be necessary, technical cooperation among developing countries (TCDC) is becoming increasingly important. Technologies passed from one developing country to another may work better than those evolved in the developed world.

Channels for technology transfer include regional centres for integrated development in the Near East (CARDNE), Asia and the Pacific (CIRDAP) and Africa (CIRDAFRICA); technical cooperation networks (in 1994 there were some 25 of them linked to institutions in Latin America and the Caribbean); and global information networks, such as AGRIS/CARIS, set up by FAO to provide information on agricultural research and technology. By mid-1995, 73 countries and 2 700 experts were participating in AGRIS/CARIS.

Examples of TCDC include:
• The adoption of Asian equipment by rice growers in the Sahel. This includes push rotary hoes and weeders, for swift weeding, and a stove developed in Viet Nam which burns rice husks. By burning hitherto unused

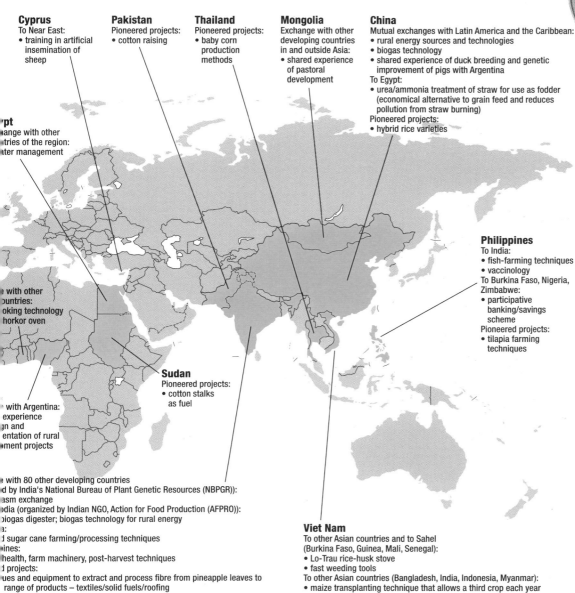

Cyprus
To Near East:
• training in artificial insemination of sheep

Pakistan
Pioneered projects:
• cotton raising

Thailand
Pioneered projects:
• baby corn production methods

Mongolia
Exchange with other developing countries in and outside Asia:
• shared experience of pastoral development

China
Mutual exchanges with Latin America and the Caribbean:
• rural energy sources and technologies
• biogas technology
• shared experience of duck breeding and genetic improvement of pigs with Argentina
To Egypt:
• urea/ammonia treatment of straw for use as fodder (economical alternative to grain feed and reduces pollution from straw burning)
Pioneered projects:
• hybrid rice varieties

...pt
...ange with other
...tries of the region:
...ter management

...e with other
...ountries:
...oking technology
...horkor oven

Sudan
Pioneered projects:
• cotton stalks as fuel

...with Argentina:
...experience
...gn and
...entation of rural
...ment projects

...with 80 other developing countries
...d by India's National Bureau of Plant Genetic Resources (NBPGR)):
...asm exchange
...ndia (organized by Indian NGO, Action for Food Production (AFPRO)):
...biogas digester; biogas technology for rural energy
...a:
...d sugar cane farming/processing techniques
...ines:
...health, farm machinery, post-harvest techniques
...d projects:
...ues and equipment to extract and process fibre from pineapple leaves to
...range of products – textiles/solid fuels/roofing

Philippines
To India:
• fish-farming techniques
• vaccinology
To Burkina Faso, Nigeria, Zimbabwe:
• participative banking/savings scheme
Pioneered projects:
• tilapia farming techniques

Viet Nam
To other Asian countries and to Sahel (Burkina Faso, Guinea, Mali, Senegal):
• Lo-Trau rice-husk stove
• fast weeding tools
To other Asian countries (Bangladesh, India, Indonesia, Myanmar):
• maize transplanting technique that allows a third crop each year

The UN Conference on Environment and Development – the Earth Summit – in 1992 placed technology transfer on the international agenda as an essential factor in development programmes.

The map (left) shows some selected examples of technical cooperation among developing countries.

New technology using waste materials is spreading throughout the developing world. Lo-Trau stove fuelled by rice husks (top). Meal cooked using biogas made in the family's own yard using fermented organic waste (bottom).

residues from rice mills, the stoves reduce pressure on forests for fuelwood and charcoal. They produce no smoke, and the ash can be used as fertilizer.

● The transfer of a model biogas digester from India to Cambodia. The digester was developed for use in India by a local NGO, Action for Food Production (AFPRO), which has now adapted it for Cambodia, where deforestation has been exacerbated by two decades of social upheaval.

● An agreement between India and the Philippines which provides for study visits, consultancies and the exchange of information and germplasm. The two countries are engaged in training each others' technicians in a wide range of fields. These include fish farming and vaccinology (from the Philippines to India), and animal health, farm machinery and the post-harvest treatment of cashew nuts (from India to the Philippines).

● A regional workshop in Buenos Aires in 1992, attended by 19 Latin American and Caribbean countries and China, Nigeria and the Philippines. Over 270 joint projects were agreed. They included Guatemalan training of Argentinians in control of the cattle worm; Argentinian help to Nigeria on potato and sunflower production and marketing; Chilean advice to China on wine production; and the transfer of an ancient Inca method of preserving potatoes from Peru to Guatemala, Cuba and Colombia.

A question of commitment

World food security depends on increased, and above all, better directed investment in agricultural development in the developing world. This requires greater commitment from both developed and developing countries.

Official aid to agriculture in the developing countries rose from some US$ 11 000 million a year in the early 1980s to US$ 14 000 million in 1988 – but has now plummeted to less than US$ 10 000 million a year in today's values. The private sector, including farm households, provides 80 percent of all investment. Public spending on agriculture within developing countries has also fallen. It is difficult to calculate exactly how much is spent every year, but FAO data suggest that between 1977 and 1992 some US$ 26 000 million a year was invested in on-farm improvements and some US$ 16 000 million a year in post-harvest facilities and in agro-industry.

Estimates suggest that the level of net investment will not have to increase much, in most of the world, to meet the needs of the next two decades: the exception is sub-Saharan Africa, where investment must double. However, gross investment, including capital stock maintenance, needs to grow by about US$ 39 000 million a year in primary and post-production operations. Of this, US$ 5 000 million must be spent on rural infrastructure and social services, which have been neglected by both national governments and donors. Less than 10 percent of the US$ 200 000 million spent on infrastructure in the developing world in 1993

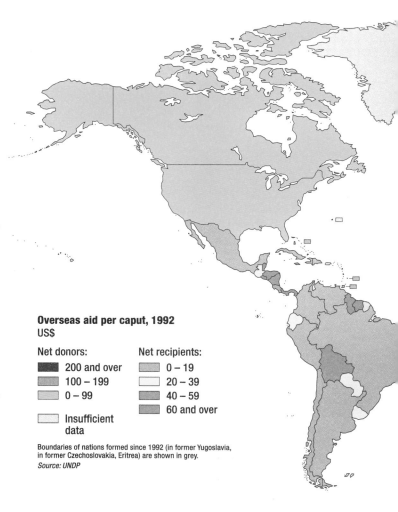

Overseas aid per caput, 1992
US$

Net donors:
- ■ 200 and over
- ■ 100 – 199
- ■ 0 – 99
- □ Insufficient data

Net recipients:
- 0 – 19
- 20 – 39
- 40 – 59
- 60 and over

Boundaries of nations formed since 1992 (in former Yugoslavia, in former Czechoslovakia, Eritrea) are shown in grey.
Source: UNDP

went to the countryside.

Priorities for investment have shifted in recent years as a result of diminishing per caput availability of land, environmental concerns and a greater focus on people and poverty. Future needs include the development of new technology; intensification (via irrigation, land improvement, mechanization and the use of purchased inputs); the improvement or construction of facilities to handle, store, process, transport and market produce; and the improvement of rural roads, power supplies and telecommunications. These priorities vary from

region to region. In Asia and Latin America, for example, rapid urban growth calls for relatively large investment in marketing and processing. In Africa, rural infrastructure is a top priority.

Issues such as locust and desertification control, early warning systems for drought and famines, outbreaks of plant and animal disease, and shared fishery and water resources involve more than one country at a time. Investment is particularly weak and difficult to organize unless the countries concerned are committed to finding solutions.

Development patterns that perpetuate today's inequities are neither sustainable nor worth sustaining.

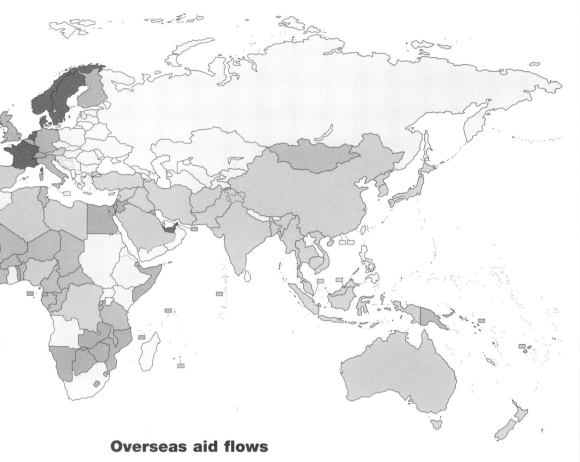

Overseas aid flows

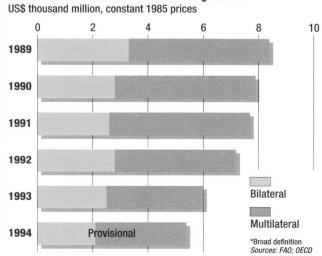

Assistance to agriculture

Commitments of external assistance to agriculture*
US$ thousand million, constant 1985 prices

	0	2	4	6	8	10
1989						
1990						
1991						
1992						
1993						
1994	Provisional					

☐ Bilateral

■ Multilateral

*Broad definition
Sources: FAO; OECD

Participation

Members of the village committee of Ankofafa, Madagascar, inspect the results of community anti-erosion measures.

Small farmers are the major agents of agricultural improvement in the developing world. They invest their savings and labour; they have the most to lose or gain from the projects designed by governments or aid agencies. Their commitment is vital to any success.

In the past, city-based experts and planners have tended to overlook grassroots opinion and expertise. FAO's Investment Centre (IC) helps potential borrowers to design projects for investment by donors and has placed great importance in recent years on involving farmers in the process. This makes it

possible to tailor projects to farmers' needs and to establish what innovations they are prepared to adopt.

In Zaire, for example, collaboration between farmers and peasant organizations has helped strengthen agricultural extension in six pilot areas of the country. A wide variety of farmer-driven and government-supported initiatives in agricultural training have enabled an estimated 320 000 farmers to be reached over a five-year period. The farmers were trained in areas such as agroforestry, market gardening and animal husbandry. Similar work in China has led to nearly US$ 1 000 million worth of projects. Further projects are starting in Armenia, Jordan, Mali and Zambia.

Indicators of rural poverty

■ Rural population as percentage of total population
■ Rural poor as percentage of total poor

Source: World Bank

Selected developing countries:

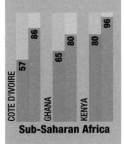

COTE D'IVOIRE 57
GHANA 65 / 86
KENYA 80 / 80 / 96

Sub-Saharan Africa

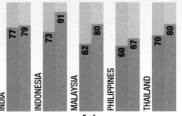

INDIA 77 / 79
INDONESIA 73 / 91
MALAYSIA 62 / 80
PHILIPPINES 60 / 67
THAILAND 70 / 80

Asia

GUATEMALA 59 / 66
MEXICO 31 / 37
PANAMA 50 / 59
PERU 44 / 52
VENEZUELA 15 / 20

Latin America

Food and Agriculture: the Future

Dimensions of Need

The right to food

The most basic of human rights is the right to adequate food and nutrition.

No human right is more fundamental than the right to food. Other human rights mean relatively little to those who are starving. Yet, although the world has enough food for all – and its average availability per caput has increased over the past three decades – some 800 million people are still chronically malnourished. Although the diets needed to provide the nutrients essential for a healthy and productive life are known, an estimated 2 000 million people still suffer from micronutrient deficiency diseases.

The United Nations, since its inception, has insisted that access to adequate food is a universal human right and a collective responsibility of the world community. In 1948 the Universal Declaration of Human Rights recognized that "everyone has the right to a standard of living adequate for the health and well-being of himself and his family, including food…". In 1966, the International Covenant on Economic, Social and Cultural Rights developed this more explicitly, stressing the "right of everyone to… adequate food" and specifying that everyone's fundamental right is to be free of hunger. The same rights were reaffirmed at the 1974 World Food Conference.

FAO's Constitution clearly sets out its intention of

FAO seeks to mobilize international and national support for the establishment of world food security.

ensuring humanity's freedom from hunger and calls on governments to take action, individually and collectively, to help to bring this about. The Organization looks beyond promoting food production to examining conditions for a stable food supply and to aiming to ensure that everyone always has both physical and economic access to basic food needs. In 1983 the FAO Conference adopted three key guidelines for world food security: ensuring adequate food availability; providing access to food, particularly for

the poor; and enhancing the stability of food supplies. FAO continues to press for wider recognition of the right to food and, in 1992, it initiated the Declaration of Barcelona which emphasizes food rights and seeks to mobilize support from international organizations, governments, non-governmental organizations and individuals. This right to food found a practical expression in the Plan of Action adopted by the joint FAO/WHO International Conference on Nutrition in 1992.

Agriculture in the twenty-first century

As we progress into the next century, the world as a whole will continue to produce enough to feed an increasing population. Nutrition will continue to improve in most developing regions. But the disparities between regions will become even greater, with sub-Saharan Africa particularly badly affected.

The rate of growth in world food production, which has been slowing down for the past three decades, will continue to decelerate. It dropped from 3 percent a year in the 1960s to 2 percent in the 1980s, and is expected to continue to fall to 1.8 percent in 2010. World population, meanwhile, is forecast to increase to around 7 000 million, 94 percent of the increase being in developing countries.

Food supplies for direct human consumption will increase in developing countries from about 2 500 calories per caput per day in the early 1990s to just over 2 700 calories in 2010. By then three regions – East Asia (including China), North Africa and the Near East, and Latin America and the Caribbean – are likely to reach or exceed the 3 000 calorie mark. South Asia may make significant progress, coming close to the present developing country average. But in sub-Saharan Africa – where nutrition has already declined over the past three decades – food supplies per caput are likely to grow little, if at all, remaining at less than 2 200 calories a day.

As a result, sub-Saharan Africa is likely to take over from South Asia as the region with the greatest number of chronically undernourished people; the number is expected to grow there from 200 million at the start of the 1990s to around 300 million 20 years later, while the number in South Asia is expected to fall only marginally from the present 250 million. These broad estimates indicate there may be fewer chronically malnourished in the developing world, despite population growth: down from the present 800 million to 650 million. But this estimate shows that past hopes that the world would be on a firm path to eliminating hunger and malnutrition by the end of the century remain optimistic in the absence of any new, major global initiative that might significantly change present perspectives.

Total imports of agricultural products by developing countries are growing faster than exports. For some, this will reflect the development process as they turn away from economies dominated by agriculture. But for those low-income countries that remain heavily dependent on agricultural exports to finance food and other imports it will reduce their chances for sustainable economic growth.

The future, just like the past, is likely to be characterized by a mix of successes and failures along the path towards a better fed world and more sustainable livelihoods and agriculture.

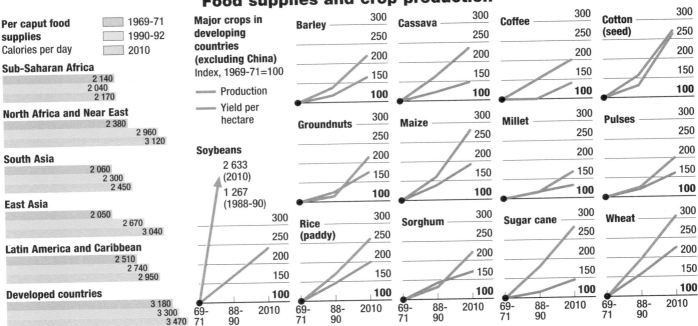

Food supplies and crop production

Per caput food supplies
Calories per day

- 1969-71
- 1990-92
- 2010

Sub-Saharan Africa
2 140
2 040
2 170

North Africa and Near East
2 380
2 960
3 120

South Asia
2 060
2 300
2 450

East Asia
2 050
2 670
3 040

Latin America and Caribbean
2 510
2 740
2 950

Developed countries
3 180
3 300
3 470

Major crops in developing countries (excluding China)
Index, 1969-71=100

— Production
— Yield per hectare

Soybeans
2 633 (2010)
1 267 (1988-90)

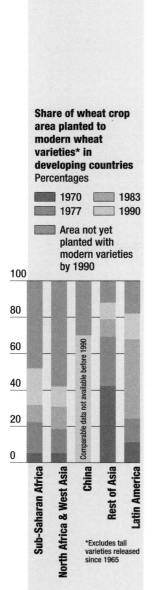

Share of wheat crop area planted to modern wheat varieties* in developing countries
Percentages

Forecasts suggest that by 2010, agriculture will tend to be more intensive and more productive.

Increasing yields

Increases in food production by the year 2010 will depend on further intensification of agriculture in developing countries. Together with growth in yields, more land will be brought into production and the existing land used more intensively.

Growth in yields has been the main cause of increases in production in the past, and will be even more important in the future, particularly in Asia and North Africa and the Near East, where land is scarce. Yields of both wheat and rice are expected to grow substantially, if less rapidly than in the past, but this will depend on an unabated research effort.

Fertilizer use in developing countries (excluding China) has grown four-fold over the past 20 years, although the rate of growth declined sharply from the 1970s to the 1980s. Application is expected to go on increasing, while the rate of growth will continue to fall: it is forecast that some 80 million tonnes of nutrients in the form of fertilizer will be used in developing countries, outside China, in 2010, compared to 37 million tonnes in the early 1990s.

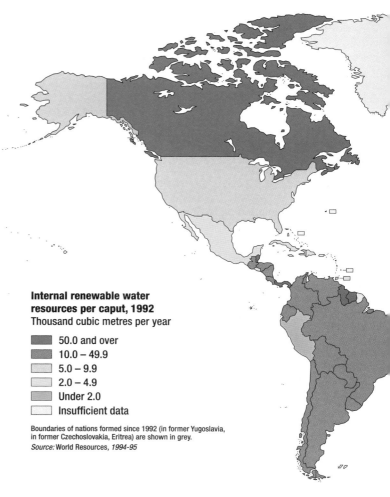

Internal renewable water resources per caput, 1992
Thousand cubic metres per year

- 50.0 and over
- 10.0 – 49.9
- 5.0 – 9.9
- 2.0 – 4.9
- Under 2.0
- Insufficient data

Boundaries of nations formed since 1992 (in former Yugoslavia, in former Czechoslovakia, Eritrea) are shown in grey.
Source: World Resources, *1994-95*

The amount of land under cultivation is expected to increase. In 1995 about 760 million hectares were used to produce crops in the least developed countries (excluding China): this could grow to some 850 million hectares by 2010. Only about 600 million of the 760 million hectares in use are actually cropped and harvested in an average year – a cropping intensity of 79 percent. This rate of use could increase to 85 percent, bringing the total harvested area to some 720 million hectares by 2010.

The area occupied by human settlements could increase by some 35 million hectares, some of which will be land with agricultural potential. The expansion would take place mainly in sub-Saharan Africa and Latin America and the Caribbean, although there might also be some in East Asia (excluding China).

Achieving higher yields and greater intensification will depend crucially on maintaining and expanding irrigation systems; they will have to increase by 23 million hectares, or 19 percent, over and above the area lost to waterlogging and salinization. The bulk of this increase would be in South Asia.

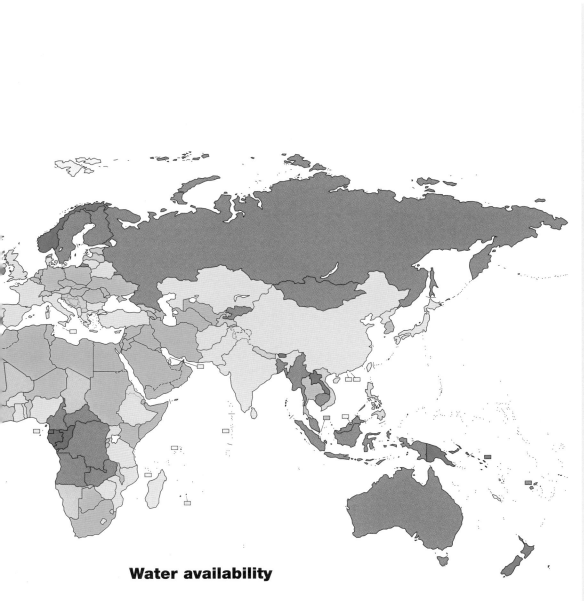

Water availability

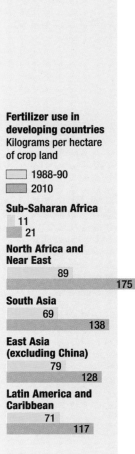

Fertilizer use in developing countries
Kilograms per hectare of crop land

- 1988-90
- 2010

Sub-Saharan Africa
11
21

North Africa and Near East
89
175

South Asia
69
138

East Asia (excluding China)
79
128

Latin America and Caribbean
71
117

Sustainable production

Working towards eliminating undernutrition and food insecurity in developing countries is only one of the two main tasks that have to be undertaken in order to feed present and future generations. The other is the need to safeguard the productive potential and broader environmental functions of agricultural resources.

The FAO Forest Resources Assessment of tropical countries in 1990 estimated their annual deforestation to be about 15.4 million hectares or 0.8 percent of the total tropical forest area. Agricultural expansion is a major contributor to deforestation and is expected to continue to be so. The impact of the expansion of crop production need not be great. More deforestation is likely to continue, however, as a result of the extension of grazing and of informal, unrecorded – often slash-and-burn – agriculture. Both deforestation and the draining of wetlands for agriculture will reduce biological diversity.

Water

Demand for water is expected to grow in years to come, but Africa and Asia are already experiencing an increasing shortage in the availability of water per caput. In many countries throughout the world water resources are scarcer than land availability. The need to increase agricultural production will accentuate pressures on water; the resulting scarcity may drive up prices beyond economic levels for crops in some areas. Meanwhile over-extraction of groundwater, particularly in the Near East and large areas of South Asia, is causing water levels to fall beneath the reach of the shallow tubewells used for irrigation, or leading to intrusions of salt water which

In the future, the current problems of water distribution and resource and environmental degradation are likely to increase.

make it unsuitable for crop production. Water contamination from a number of sources including fertilizers, pesticides and the effluents of intensive livestock units and fish farms, is likely to increase.

The problem of land degradation is also likely to grow. Degradation from "nutrient mining" – denuding soils of major nutrients such as nitrogen and phosphorus and micronutrients such as boron and manganese – is serious in many countries, but most acute in sub-Saharan Africa.

Poverty is a major driving force behind rural environmental damage, as more and more people try to extract a living out of dwindling resources, producing a risk of a vicious circle of human deprivation and resource degradation. But it is not exclusively to blame.

Wealthier areas of the world, such as Western Europe and North America, have also suffered resource degradation, including soil erosion, water pollution and deforestation. They have responded, in part, by changing policies and incentives and by increasing investment. Most important of all, they have devised technological options and innovation and have educated land users in how to protect the resource base while increasing productivity. This is the same challenge facing many developing countries today.

Rural poverty

Reducing and eliminating rural poverty is the most effective way both to tackle hunger and to promote development, concludes the FAO study *World Agriculture: Towards 2010.* It says, "Only a combination of faster, poverty reducing development and public policy, both national and international, will ultimately improve access to food by the poor and eliminate chronic undernutrition."

Increasing agricultural production as such will not end hunger since poor people may not be able to afford to buy the food that is produced; increasing the output in countries highly dependent on agriculture will, however, boost rural incomes and thus reduce poverty and assist development, since most of the world's poorest people depend on agriculture as the main source of their income.

Policies that neglected agriculture and promoted inappropriate technologies and management practices are now discredited. The FAO study calls for the shifting of technology from such "hardware" solutions as large doses of pesticides or building terraces with machines, to "solutions based on more sophisticated, knowledge and information-intensive resource management practices which can lower both off-farm costs and environmental pressures". New policies and institutional measures will be needed to help farmers, forest users and fisherfolk pursue sustainable agricultural and rural development.

Access to land, through land reform, is a major factor in poverty alleviation and agricultural growth. Progress so far has been limited, but the case for reform remains strong on both efficiency and equity grounds. The poor in agriculture need better access to rural finance and better marketing services. And they need education, training and technical assistance to help them to be open to the new and profitable innovations that will be especially necessary in the transition to sustainable development. In this there is a role both for direct government intervention and for private sector initiatives.

Rural illiteracy rates
Percentages

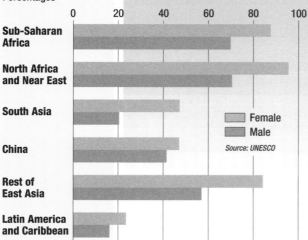

Source: UNESCO

Sharing the world's resources

Less than one-quarter of the world's people, those who live in the developed countries of both West and East, consume 80 percent of the energy and metals and 85 percent of the paper used each year. Three countries, the United States, Germany and Japan, together produce more than half of the planet's economic output, while the 450 million people of sub-Saharan Africa share about the same amount as the 10 million who live in Belgium.

The high consumption and high productivity of the industrialized countries need to be balanced by a shift in investment, research and development, productive capacity, and management and other skills to the developing world. At the same time, the developed countries need to become more efficient by reducing waste and paying the full price of goods and raw materials imported from developing countries.

The intensive use of energy by the industrialized countries causes pollution and contributes to global warming, while the overnutrition of many of their people causes disease and death. Poverty in many developing countries leads people to cut down forests, damage watersheds and degrade the land, while undernutrition also kills and gravely damages health. A more equitable sharing of resources would assist development and help reduce critical pressures on the environment in developed and developing countries alike.

The 1992 UN Conference on Environment and Development, the Earth Summit, focused world attention on sustainability and natural resources, and set out in Agenda 21 a plan of action for future global partnerships. FAO played a major role in drafting Agenda 21 and has been designated the "task manager" for following up many of its resolutions.

The Organization's primary responsibilities cover land resources, forests, mountain ecosystems, and sustainable agriculture and rural development. But it is also involved in water resources, control of desertification, conservation of biological diversity, oceans and coastal issues, and the provision of information for decision making. FAO promotes joint activities and programmes to

The richest quarter of the world's population accounts for more than three-quarters of consumption of many natural resources. At the other end of the spectrum, the poor satisfy their immediate needs by destroying their local resources – slash-and-burn agriculture, Mexico (below).

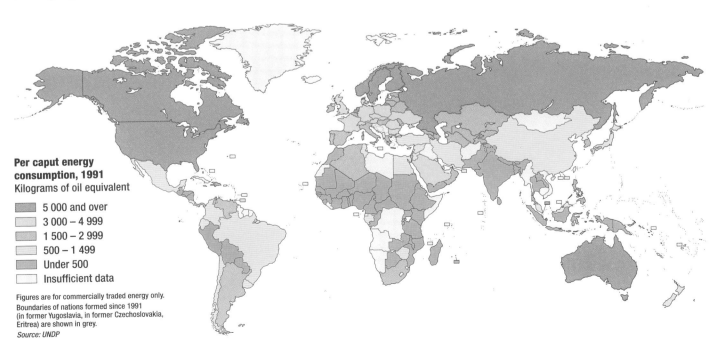

Per caput energy consumption, 1991
Kilograms of oil equivalent

- 5 000 and over
- 3 000 – 4 999
- 1 500 – 2 999
- 500 – 1 499
- Under 500
- Insufficient data

Figures are for commercially traded energy only.
Boundaries of nations formed since 1991
(in former Yugoslavia, in former Czechoslovakia,
Eritrea) are shown in grey.
Source: UNDP

Terraced farmland, Nepal. FAO supports many programmes designed to meet the particular needs of mountain areas such as this, and their inhabitants.

Diagnosing information for sound decision making is a major objective of Agenda 21. FAO is developing indicators of sustainable agriculture and rural development (SARD) for a number of areas including forest management (with the International Tropical Timber Organization) and land quality (with the World Bank). It is promoting the design and application of measures to assist countries in analysing the effects of economic development on environmental and social systems.

FAO is supporting efforts to strengthen international cooperation and the exchange of information on such issues as watershed management and development of appropriate farming systems. It is helping to formulate national action plans and investment programmes; encouraging the participation of representatives from mountain communities in national development planning; and is promoting the conservation and development of the technologies and cultures of mountain areas.

FAO is assisting many countries in sustainable agricultural development. It promotes the conservation and sustainable use of plant and animal genetic resources for food and agriculture, fosters sustainable rural energy production and extends the application of integrated pest management, integrated systems for plant nutrition and other cost-effective, environment-friendly technologies. It encourages the wise use of natural resources through land and water management programmes. FAO helps to obtain investment intended to meet these objectives and direct it to resource users. It has also developed agro-ecological zone mapping, evaluating land potential and matching soils, climate and environment to crop requirements.

encourage the exchange of information, to help develop common strategies and to consolidate and analyse information for presentation to the Commission for Sustainable Development established as a result of the Earth Summit. It also chairs UN sub-committees on oceans and water resources that coordinate the implementation of the corresponding Agenda 21 chapters.

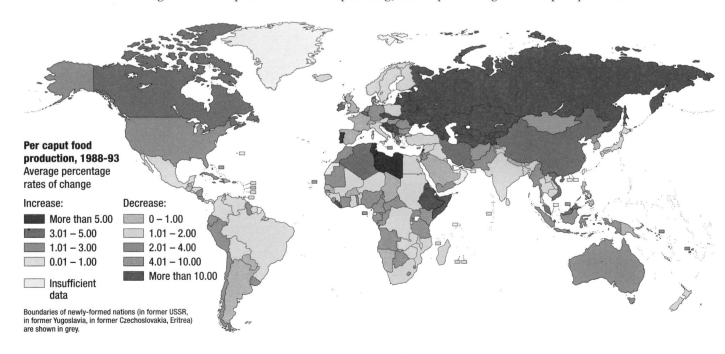

Per caput food production, 1988-93
Average percentage rates of change

Increase:
- More than 5.00
- 3.01 – 5.00
- 1.01 – 3.00
- 0.01 – 1.00
- Insufficient data

Decrease:
- 0 – 1.00
- 1.01 – 2.00
- 2.01 – 4.00
- 4.01 – 10.00
- More than 10.00

Boundaries of newly-formed nations (in former USSR, in former Yugoslavia, in former Czechoslovakia, Eritrea) are shown in grey.

Global warming

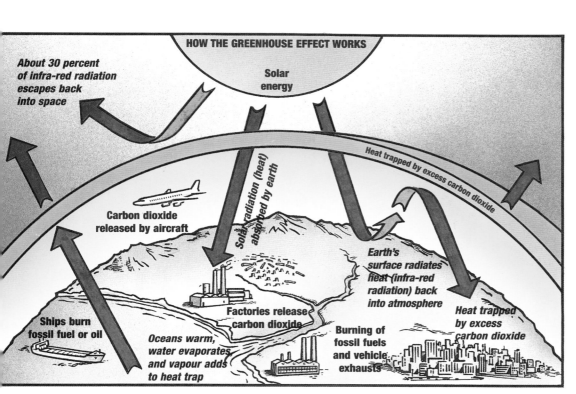

HOW THE GREENHOUSE EFFECT WORKS

Solar energy

About 30 percent of infra-red radiation escapes back into space

Heat trapped by excess carbon dioxide

Carbon dioxide released by aircraft

Solar radiation (heat) absorbed by earth

Earth's surface radiates heat (infra-red radiation) back into atmosphere

Ships burn fossil fuel or oil

Oceans warm, water evaporates and vapour adds to heat trap

Factories release carbon dioxide

Burning of fossil fuels and vehicle exhausts

Heat trapped by excess carbon dioxide

Naturally occurring greenhouse gases keep the earth warm enough to be habitable. Increasing their concentrations and adding new ones will gradually make the earth quite a different place.

Agriculture depends on the climate more than any other human activity, and so is particularly vulnerable to climatic change. The Intergovernmental Panel on Climate Change (IPCC) estimates that as a result of increasing human-induced emissions of carbon dioxide, methane, nitrous oxide and other "greenhouse gases", average temperatures may climb by about 0.3 degrees centigrade per decade over the next century, while sea levels could rise by at least 2-4 centimetres per decade. This will have an impact, still to be quantified, on agriculture, forestry, fisheries, food security, biodiversity and rural environmental conditions.

Not all of the effects of global warming would be harmful to agriculture. Higher concentrations of carbon dioxide can have a fertilizing effect under optimal growing conditions: 10-20 percent of improved crop productivity over the past century could be the result of the gradual increase in the level of the gas; and crop productivity could increase further, by up to 30 percent, if the concentration of carbon dioxide doubles as foreseen over the next 50 years. It could also offset the damage done to plant growth by other pollutants, and increase the efficiency with which crops use water. Rising temperatures could increase the yield of some plants, while diminishing others. Rainfall could also increase, by about 10 percent, but its distribution and intensity would change; some areas would benefit, others would be harmed, but it is not yet certain which ones.

Overall, global warming is expected to add to the difficulties of increasing food production. The weather and climate would become more unpredictable, making farming and planning more difficult. Present agricultural zones would shift, sometimes by hundreds of kilometres in latitude and by hundreds of metres in altitude on hills and mountains. Some plant and animal species, particularly those such as trees with long life cycles, might not be able to adjust to this and poorer farmers, in particular, would find it hard to adapt. Fishing areas may also shift, leading to disruption, although the overall productivity of the oceans might stay about the same. Diseases and pests would possibly increase. Biological diversity could be at risk in natural environments such as tropical forests and mangroves. And the rise in sea

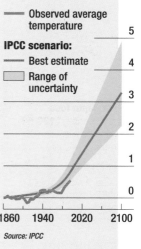

Potential changes in surface temperature according to the Intergovernmental Panel on Climate Change (IPCC)
Degrees centigrade

— Observed average temperature

IPCC scenario:
— Best estimate
▢ Range of uncertainty

5
4
3
2
1
0

1860 1940 2020 2100

Source: IPCC

According to the best estimate by the Intergovernmental Panel on Climate Change, if present trends continue, sea levels may rise by about 40 centimetres by the end of the next century. Small island states, such as the Bahamas, Maldives and Tonga, will be most affected.

Greenhouse gases

Concentration of greenhouse gases in the atmosphere
Parts per million

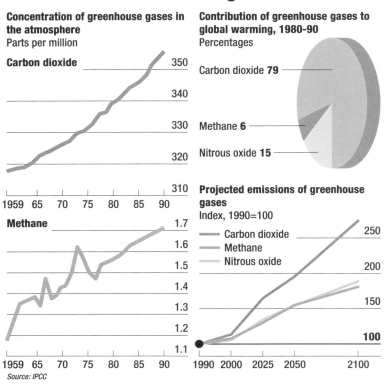

Carbon dioxide

350
340
330
320
310

1959 65 70 75 80 85 90

Methane

1.7
1.6
1.5
1.4
1.3
1.2
1.1

1959 65 70 75 80 85 90
Source: IPCC

Contribution of greenhouse gases to global warming, 1980-90
Percentages

Carbon dioxide **79**
Methane **6**
Nitrous oxide **15**

Projected emissions of greenhouse gases
Index, 1990=100

— Carbon dioxide
— Methane
— Nitrous oxide

250
200
150
100

1990 2000 2025 2050 2100

Deforestation reduces a vital store of carbon dioxide.

levels would increase flooding, submerging or waterlogging coastal plains which are among the most productive, and highly populated, lands.

Global warming is likely to accentuate the existing imbalance in world food production between the developed and developing countries. Cooler, temperate regions – home to the industrialized countries – are expected to receive most of the benefits from global warming, while tropical and subtropical ones are likely to suffer most. Farmers in wealthier countries are also most likely to be able to adapt to climate change. Sub-Saharan Africa, where food production already lags behind the rest of the world, is expected to be hardest hit.

Carbon dioxide (CO_2) is the most important greenhouse gas after water vapour. Much atmospheric CO_2 originates from use of fossil fuels for the production of energy in industrialized countries but about 30 percent has been estimated to result from deforestation and other land use practices such as rangeland burning. Some 35 percent of worldwide methane emissions are now estimated to arise from fermentation in rice paddies and in the digestive systems of cattle and other ruminants. And agriculture, including the application of nitrogenous fertilizers, may account for as much as 90 percent of nitrous oxide emissions.

The growth of carbon dioxide in the atmosphere can be slowed by reducing the rate of deforestation. Using biofuels derived from plants, instead of fossil fuels, will also reduce these emissions. Changes in land management techniques such as reforestation would stimulate the annual terrestrial uptake of atmospheric CO_2 and its storage in the organic matter of arable or grassland soils. FAO is helping governments and people to reduce emissions of methane and nitrous oxide, which have no positive effects on plant growth, by improving the use of nitrogenous fertilizer, modifying irrigated rice cultivation and feeding cattle a well-balanced diet – including, for example, straw treated with urea – that produces less methane than diets of untreated roughage.

The Organization also monitors the condition of tropical forests, helps to combat deforestation and promotes the planting of trees. It is developing plans for preparing for disasters and early warning systems for droughts, outbreaks of pests and diseases, and other "extreme events" affecting food and agriculture. It is promoting the development of more resilience in agriculture: for example, by encouraging diversification and developing improved crop varieties and animal breeds. And it is stimulating further research to assess the impact of global warming on food production.

The challenge of sustainability

"Sustainable development is pro-people, pro-jobs and pro-nature" *Human Development Report*, 1994.

There are five root causes of unsustainable agricultural practices and degradation of the rural environment:

Policy failure
Leading among the causes of unsustainable agriculture are inadequate or inappropriate policies which include pricing, subsidy and tax policies which have encouraged the excessive, and often uneconomic, use of inputs such as fertilizers and pesticides, and the overexploitation of land. They may also include policies that favour farming systems which are inappropriate both to the circumstances of the farming community and available resources.

Rural inequalities
Rural people often know best how to conserve their environment, but they may need to overexploit resources in order to survive. Meanwhile commercial exploitation by large landowners and companies often causes environmental degradation in pursuit of higher profits.

Resource imbalances
Almost all of the future growth in the world's population will be in developing countries and the biggest increases will be in the poorest countries of all, those least equipped to meet their own needs or invest in the future.

Unsustainable technologies
New technologies have boosted agricultural production worldwide, but some have had harmful side effects which must be contained and reversed, such as resistance of insects to pesticides, land degradation through wind or water erosion, nutrient depletion or poor irrigation management and the loss of biological diversity.

Trade relations
As the value of raw materials exported by developing countries has fallen, their governments have sought to boost income by expansion of crop production and timber sales that have damaged the environment.

In the long term, increasing food production depends on using natural resources sustainably, not destroying them.

Drylands

Most of the 20 million square kilometres of the world's drylands – which support 500 million people – are subject to degradation; some 60 000 square

kilometres of land are lost each year. The main strategies for sustainable agriculture and rural development must be to create employment locally and to find alternatives to practices which overexploit the land. Low-cost soil and water conservation measures are needed, while the pressure on fuelwood can be reduced by tapping other local sources of energy, such as wind and biogas. Planting legume-based crops and trees, which fix their own nitrogen, can reverse the depletion of soil nutrients and reduce the need for mineral fertilizers.

Overgrazing can be reduced by encouraging greater control over the use of resources and increasing the offtake of livestock by improving market networks. The reduction or removal of subsidies and other actions that reduce the cost of maintaining livestock can also encourage greater offtake. Growing hay, development of leguminous forage and the promotion of species of trees and shrubs that are productive during the dry season can provide alternative sources of feed and alleviate shortages.

Proposals for progress

FAO proposes a choice of four key strategies to attain sustainable agriculture and rural development. The first two promote intensification; the third and fourth are applicable when limits on natural resources or environmental or socio-economic constraints make this unsustainable.

Intensification through specialization This is mainly suited to land with high crop potential. It depends on the judicious use of external inputs such as pesticides and fertilizers combined with improved agricultural and related practices. The introduction of improved soil management, integrated pest management and efficient waste management all promote sustainability.

Intensification through diversification This is suited to a wider range of conditions. Mixed cropping systems, plus improved management techniques, help promote maximum efficiency in natural resource use. Diversification can minimize environmental and socio-economic risks, assist waste recycling and reduce the need for external inputs.

Combining on-farm and off-farm activities Promoting additional sources of income can limit pressure on natural resources.

Extensive systems Suited to marginal areas, or ones with low agricultural potential, they can either be specialized (as in ranching) or diversified (as in shifting cultivation). Few external inputs are used, so integrated pest management, water management, and the conservation and maintenance of soil fertility are particularly important. The sustainability of these systems depends on having low population densities and only light pressure on natural resources.

Three objectives should guide the choice between these options:
● improving efficiency in the use of resources and inputs;
● increasing the resilience of agriculture and producers to adverse socio-economic and environmental conditions;
● promoting diversity, through varied farming systems that help spread the farmer's risks or the use of areas for other purposes, such as forestry.

Irrigated land

About 35 percent of all irrigated land – the major source of cereals and export crops – is at risk of salinization because of poor management. Efficient use of water can be promoted by local farmers participating in drainage and irrigation design, improved training and water pricing policies that curb excessive use. Small-scale schemes planned and implemented by local institutions can reduce many irrigation problems if backed by national policies that effectively support appropriate technologies, credit, marketing, energy supplies and maintenance of equipment.

Tropical forests

Humid and semi-humid forests support 1 000 million people and are the world's largest biomass reservoir, but their sustainability is threatened by the removal of trees and the degradation of watersheds. Most of this is caused by clearing for agriculture, which is unsustainable either because the fertility of the soil is low or because the methods of cultivation are unsuitable.

To meet the needs of their increasing populations, most developing countries will need to convert some of their forest areas for agricultural use, but this needs to be done on the basis of land use planning that ensures that it is sustainable.

The pace of deforestation will be slowed only by ensuring that the conservation and management of forest resources are more attractive to local people than their destruction, and that commercial interests use forest land in a sound, sustainable way.

Options to help achieve this include agroforestry involving food crops and trees; the sustainable harvesting of non-wood forest products; and sustainable forest management and timber harvesting.

The Den Bosch Declaration

In April 1991, FAO held a conference on agriculture and the environment, with the cooperation of the Netherlands Government, attended by senior government officials and experts from some 120 countries. It adopted the Den Bosch Declaration calling for "fundamental changes" in development policies and strategies so as to meet the world's increasing need for food without degrading the environment. These changes included:

● the participation of rural people in the research and development of systems for more efficient management of the natural resources available to the farmer;
● devolving the responsibility and authority for decision making to the local level, rather than relying on "top down" administration;
● allocating clear and fair legal rights and obligations on the use of land and other natural resources, including land reforms as necessary;
● investing in improving, rehabilitating and conserving natural resources;
● adjusting economic and agricultural policies and instruments to promote production systems and technologies that can help attain sustainability;
● encouraging demand and providing incentives that favour crops and animals that can be produced and processed sustainably;
● promoting practices, production and processing systems that pay particular attention to safeguarding health and the quality of the environment;
● promoting opportunities in rural areas to earn livelihoods off the farm.

Hill and mountain areas

The world's highlands cover 10 million square kilometres, and serve as watersheds for far more. In Asia, for example, some 9 million square kilometres of downstream land is at risk of flooding as a result of highland degradation. The central objectives must be to raise farm productivity using low-cost technologies, and to reduce population pressure. Policies that promote employment in agriculture and opportunities for income outside it are recommended. Perennial tree and shrub crops, and mixing crops and livestock, provide sustainable alternatives to shifting agriculture and produce higher incomes from far less land.

Sustainable forest management and agroforestry provide fodder, fuelwood and timber, and reduce erosion. Moderate slopes should be reserved for horticultural and fodder crops, steep ones for tree crops – possibly through incentives and regulations. Overgrazing can be countered by selling more livestock, sterilization and culling, and controlling livestock by stall feeding. Improved breeds and animal health will raise productivity, even with fewer animals.

As these areas often have poor access, their management relies on local initiatives, but these must be complemented by development of roads, hydropower schemes, and better credit and marketing.

Fair and free trade

It is often assumed that agricultural trade liberalization will benefit developing countries, but the regions that will benefit most, in the short term, from the GATT Agreement on Agriculture are among the richest in the world.

The Uruguay Round of the General Agreement on Tariffs and Trade (GATT), concluded in December 1993, is the first to include the liberalization of agricultural trade. Its Agreement on Agriculture could cut tariffs by an average of 36 percent in developed countries and 24 percent in developing ones and reduce domestic support for producers by 20 percent and 13.3 percent respectively. Expenditure on export subsidies is to be cut by 36 percent. Developing countries have ten years in which to make the cuts, compared with six for developed countries; the least developed are not required to make any reductions at all.

Food prices will rise and this will, naturally, benefit exporters and hurt importing countries. But farmers in developing countries may also gain because subsidized exports from developed countries have undercut them, reducing production. For the same reason, the food security of developing countries should also improve. There should be some reduction in agricultural production in the developed countries and a slight rise in the developing ones, but the total world harvest will hardly be affected.

In all, the value of world agricultural trade is expected to rise by about 1 percent. Half of this will result from higher prices, half from increases in volume. The Agreement is likely to slow down the general decline in the growth rate of world trade seen since the 1980s – caused mainly by decreased imports by the main developed countries – but it seems unlikely to halt it.

In fact, the impact of the Agreement is expected to be comparatively small since it represents only partial liberalization. The cuts in support to agriculture, although impressive in absolute numbers of dollars, are relatively small and are spread over a number of years. Even after the changes have been completed, a large degree of distortion will remain in the market. The Agreement calls for the process of liberalization to continue with the long-term objective of "substantial progressive reductions in support and protection, resulting in fundamental reform".

The regions that will benefit most from the Agreement on Agriculture are among the richest in the world, while many developing countries, particularly in Africa, are likely to lose from it.

The implications for individual countries of FAO's projections for agricultural commodity markets following the implementation of the Uruguay Round stem from changes in market prices, new opportunities for exports and the extent to which external markets may influence producers and consumers.

Exports of developed countries in the year 2000 would be some US$ 17 000 million higher as a result of the Agreement on Agriculture and those of developing countries would increase by some US$ 9 300 million. At the same time, imports of developed countries are projected to increase by about US$ 19 000 million compared with an increase of US$ 6 400 million for developing countries. The major

beneficiaries are the great food exporting regions of North America, the Southwest Pacific and Latin America.

Developing countries will face considerable changes in world market conditions, and they will be hurt by a side-effect of liberalization: the erosion in the value of the preferences that industrialized countries give to produce from some developing countries. The agricultural preferences given by the European Union, Japan and the United States in 1992 were potentially worth US$ 1 900 million; this is expected to fall by nearly half (US$ 800 million) as a result of the Uruguay Round. Many of the recipients of such preferential schemes are among the poorest developing countries.

Most African countries tend to be importers of food, particularly wheat, rice and

The present net surplus in the agricultural trade balance of developing countries is likely to decrease in the future.

FOOD AND AGRICULTURE: THE FUTURE DIMENSIONS OF NEED

Under the GATT Agreement on Agriculture, food prices will rise on the world markets. This will favour exporting countries but also offers importing countries an opportunity to reward their farmers and reduce imports.

promotes diversification in their export crops. The rise in world prices and decrease in export subsidies offers them an opportunity to reward their farmers better in order to encourage greater production.

Much of Asia is largely self-sufficient in food and its agricultural exports are expected to increase as a result of the Agreement. In Latin America and the Caribbean a rise in agricultural export earnings is expected to outweigh greatly the increase in the cost of food imports, so that the region's favourable balance of trade should rise from US$ 20 000 million in 1987-89 to US$ 32 000 million in the year 2000: US$ 2 400 million of this estimated increase is ascribed to the Uruguay Round.

dairy products, and exporters of tropical products such as cocoa, coffee and fruit and some agricultural raw materials. Twenty-eight of them are among the least developed and 44 are among the low-income food-deficit countries. The increases in the price of food from temperate areas as a result of the Agreement are likely to cause a substantial rise in their import bills; the value of their exports would also rise but not by so much. Estimates suggest that their US$ 1 000 million export surplus in all agricultural commodities in 1987-89 will become a deficit of US$ 500 million in the year 2000, partly as a result of the Uruguay Round.

Most African countries could well have to give greater weight to a strategy that increases food production and

Probable evolution of net agricultural trade balance

	Net balance (US$ million) 1988/90	Likely changes 1988/90-2010 (percent)		Net balance (US$ million) 1988/90	Likely changes 1988/90-2010 (percent)
Coffee	+7 544	+24	Pulses	-194	+100 or more
Oilseeds, vegetable oils, oil-meals	+3 640	+50	Cotton, excl. cotton textiles	-265	increase, probably large
Sugar	+3 244	decline	Animal fats	-689	increase
Rubber	+2 924	+35	Wool, excl. wool textiles	-917	increase, probably large
Cocoa	+2 211	+24			
Citrus	+1 659	+10-20	Beverages (mostly alcoholic)	-952	increase
Bananas	+1 927	+33			
Other fruit	+1 989	+100-150	Meat, eggs	-1 137	+100 or more
Vegetables	+1 756	+50-70	Hides and skins, excl. leather products	-1 547	increase, probably large
Tea	+1 055	+20			
Spices	+570	modest increase	Dairy products	-5 348	+55
Cassava/other roots	+899	-40	Cereals	-15 962	+80
Vegetable fibres, excl. cotton	+91	0 or decline			
Tobacco	+8	0			
Other products (unspecified)	+2 498				
Sub-total	**+32 015**		**Sub-total**	**-27 011**	
			NET BALANCE	**+5 004**	

Tapping the peace dividend

World military spending in 1992 (US$ 815 000 million) equalled the income of 49 percent of the world's people

Total world income

Total world military spending

There were hopes when the Cold War came to an end that reductions in arms expenditure, in both developed and developing countries, would release large sums for investment in development. This has still to happen.

Global military spending has fallen sharply – from a peak of US$ 995 000 million in 1987 to US$ 767 000 million in 1994 (at constant 1991 prices). This cut, an average of 4 percent a year over the period, yielded a saving of US$ 935 000 million. But little of it has been spent on human or sustainable development. The United States and the countries of the former Soviet Union have led the way in reducing spending, but in the former most of the savings have gone to reduce the overall budget deficit and national debt, while in the latter they have been largely swallowed up in economic crisis.

The potential for tapping the peace dividend, however, remains. Military spending still places a large burden on the world's resources and is equal to the total income of almost half the world's people. The 1994 *Human Development Report* estimated that a further 12 percent reduction would release enough money to provide safe drinking water and primary health care (including the immunization of children) for the entire world population, eliminate severe undernutrition and cut moderate undernutrition by half. An earlier report estimated that continuing to reduce military spending by a further 3-4 percent a year while earmarking one-quarter of the savings for aid, would raise official development

assistance to meet the UN target of 0.7 percent of GNP and still leave a substantial amount to spare for use at home.

Considerable scope also exists for tapping the peace dividend by cutting military expenditure in developing countries. Their spending rose by 7.5 percent a year between 1960 and 1987, almost three times as fast as in developed countries, while their share in global expenditure more than doubled from 7 percent to 15 percent. So far they have undertaken little disarmament.

The establishment of a Global Demilitarization Fund

under international jurisdiction has been proposed by Oscar Arias, the former President of Costa Rica and winner of the 1987 Nobel Peace Prize. He suggests using a proportion of the peace dividend to achieve further cuts in expenditures. All countries would commit themselves to reducing military spending by at least 3 percent a year: developed ones would give perhaps one-fifth, and developing countries perhaps one-tenth, of their savings to the Fund. This would then be used to reward the efforts primarily, but not exclusively, of developing countries to disarm and demobilize.

The peace dividend

Global military expenditures and the peace dividend
US$ thousand million, 1991 prices and exchange rates

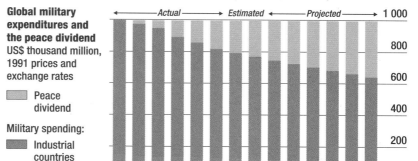

◻	Peace dividend	
Military spending:		
▨	Industrial countries	
▨	Developing countries	

Actual → Estimated ← Projected →

1987 88　90　92　94　96　98　2000

Total military spending in developing countries, 1992

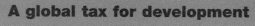

US$ 125 000 million

8 percent of military spending:
Would provide a basic family planning package to all willing couples and stabilize world population by the year 2015.

12 percent of military spending:
Would provide primary health care for all, including immunization of all children, elimination of severe malnutrition and reduction of moderate malnutrition by half, and provision of safe drinking water for all.

4 percent of military spending:
Would reduce adult illiteracy by half, provide universal primary education and educate women to the same level as men.

Source: Human Development Report, *1994*

A global tax for development

As official aid shrinks, development experts are proposing new ways of raising the money to fund development. These could be less dependent on the changing priorities of donor countries and their governments. Many envisage new forms of international taxation.

A global income tax has been proposed, as has a world tax on the use of such shared resources as the oceans (for fishing, transport or mining seabed minerals), the Antarctic (for mining) or space (for communications satellites). There are also various proposals for pollution taxes, particularly on emissions of carbon dioxide, the main contributor to global warming: some

countries already have domestic carbon taxes in place.

Professor James Tobin (left), winner of the 1981 Nobel Prize for Economic Sciences, has proposed a worldwide tax on international currency transactions, which now amount to US$ 1 000 000 million a day. A levy of just 0.5 percent on each transaction would raise over US$ 1 500 000 million a year. He says that such a tax would slow down speculative movements of capital, while not being heavy enough to deter commodity trade or serious international capital commitments. The proceeds would be devoted to international purposes and placed at the disposal of international institutions.

Promises to keep

The Constitution of FAO is as relevant now as when it was adopted 50 years ago. The promises made then have still to be met in full, but considerable progress has been made in alleviating hunger and poverty. The availability of food set against the total population of the world has increased even though the population has more than doubled. World agricultural production and international trade in agricultural products have grown dramatically. There have been broad gains in the standard of living in terms of income, health and education.

Despite these gains, millions of people, mainly in developing countries, still lack the food that they need for a healthy, productive and active life. At the same time, because the benefits of past progress have not been shared equitably, the gap between rich and poor, individuals and nations alike, has grown wider. Global food security, which will ensure that everyone has an adequate diet, has yet to be put in place.

The population of the world at the time of FAO's founding stood at about 2 500 million persons. By FAO's 50th Anniversary in 1995, it had reached an estimated 5 700 million. In 2045, the Population Division of the United Nations has projected that it could be between 7 960 million and 11 316 million, according to whether one assumes a low or high growth rate for the years to come. No matter which scenario may prove the more accurate, one thing is certain: in the foreseeable future our planet must sustain an increasing number of people, bringing an even greater demand for food, clothing, shelter, health care and education.

The existence of poverty and hunger is the principal challenge facing the world community. As the specialized agency responsible within the United Nations system for food, agriculture and rural development, FAO clearly has a central role in helping meet these challenges. In fact, the elimination of hunger and the establishment of food security by means of sustainable development are the driving forces underlying the mission of the Organization as it moves towards a new century.

In celebrating the 50th Anniversary of FAO, its Members have chosen to reaffirm their dedication to its principles and to renew their commitment to its mission. Setting objectives for food, agriculture and rural development, and the conservation of natural resources, this partnership, which embraces almost every nation in the world, has agreed to give due emphasis to:
● promoting agriculture, forestry and fisheries as key sectors in the quest for sustainable economic development;
● empowering food producers and consumers, recognizing the importance of those who harvest the earth's natural resources and the rights of all people to safe, nutritious food;
● making sustainable use of natural resources for development thereby meeting the responsibility as custodians of this heritage to present and future generations;
● building a global development partnership in which all nations and peoples can participate in order to achieve growth with equity.

Management and sustainable use of natural resources is vital.

A favourable environment for trade needs to be created.

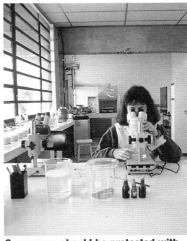

Consumers should be protected with safe, good quality foods.

FAO has seen 50 years of progress yet its pursuit of a better and more equitable world is unchanged.

Using natural resources can provide jobs and incomes to combat poverty.

Food losses can be minimized by improving storage and preservation.

All people, particularly women, should be able to participate fully in rural development.

Sustainable use and care of natural resources should be rewarded.

Research capacity must be strengthened in developing countries.

Food security and improved nutritional status for everyone should be a priority in national policies and plans.

INDEX

FURTHER INFORMATION

PUBLISHED IN ROME BY FAO

1984
Land, Food and People.

1984
Sharing Experience for Progress.

1985
Fifth World Food Survey.

1986
Introduction to Irrigation.

1989
Fertilizers and Food Production.

1989
Forestry and Nutrition – a Reference Manual.

1989
Nuclear Strategies in Food and Agriculture, 1964-1989.

1989
Sustainable Agricultural Production: Implications for International Agricultural Research.

1990
The Conservation and Rehabilitation of African Lands.

1991
FAO/Netherlands Conference on Agriculture and the Environment, Report of the Conference.

1991
Fish for Food and Development.

1991
How Good the Earth?

1991
The Global Information and Early Warning System on Food and Agriculture.

1992
FAO Handbook on TCDC.

1992
FAO/WHO International Conference on Nutrition, Final Report of the Conference.

1992
Food and Nutrition: Creating a Well-fed World.

1992
Forests, Trees and Food.

1992
Nutrition, the Global Challenge.

1992
Protect and Produce, Putting the Pieces Together.

1992
Sustainable Development and the Environment, FAO Policies and Actions, Stockholm 1972-Rio 1992.

1993
Biotechnology in Agriculture, Forestry and Fisheries.

1993
Current World Fertilizer Situation and Outlook, 1990/91-1996/97.

1993
Food Aid in Figures, Vol II.

1993
Food and Nutrition in the Management of Group Feeding Programmes.

1993
Harvesting Nature's Diversity.

1993
Rural Poverty Alleviation: Policies and Trends.

1993
Science and Technology in the Work of FAO.

1993
World Soil Resources.

1994
Cherish the Earth.

1994
Communication: A Key to Human Development.

1994
Global Climatic Change and Agricultural Production.

1994
Water for Life.

1994
What has AIDS to do with Agriculture?

1995
Commodity Review and Outlook 1994-95.

1995
Fighting Hunger.

1995
Food Control and Consumer Protection.

1995
Food for All.

1995
Impact of the Uruguay Round on Agriculture.

1995
State of the World's Forests.

1995
The Keita Integrated Development Project.

1995
The State of World Fisheries and Aquaculture.

FAO PERIODICALS

Ceres.

DEEP (Development Education Exchange Papers).

FAO Annual Review.

Food, Nutrition and Agriculture.

Food Outlook, Global Information and Early Warning System on Food and Agriculture.

Foodcrops and Shortages.

Rural Development (RD).

TCDC (Technical and Economic Cooperation among Developing Countries) Newsletter.

The State of Food and Agriculture.

Unasylva.

Yearbook of Fishery Statistics – Catches and Landings.

Yearbook of Fishery Statistics – Commodities.

Yearbook of Forest Products.

Yearbook of Production.

Yearbook of Trade.

OTHERS

Alexandratos, N. (ed) (1995), World Agriculture: Towards 2010, An FAO Study, Chichester: Food and Agriculture Organization of the United Nations/ J. Wiley.

BP (1995), BP Statistical Review of World Energy, London: The British Petroleum Company.

Brown, L.R., Kane, H. & Roodman, D.M. (1994), *Vital Signs*, Worldwatch Institute, London & New York: W.W. Norton & Company.

CGIAR (1994), *CGIAR Annual Report 1993-1994*, Washington, D.C.: Consultative Group on International Agricultural Research.

Georghiou, G.P. & Saito, T. (1983), *Pest Resistance to Pesticides*, New York: Plenum Press.

Grigg, D. (1992), *The Transformation of Agriculture in the West*, Oxford: Blackwell.

Hoyt, E. (1992), *Conserving the Wild Relatives of Crops*, Rome: IBPGR/IUCN/WWF.

IPCC (1990), Houghton, J.T. et al. (eds), *Climate Change: The IPCC Assessment*, Cambridge: Cambridge University Press for the Intergovernmental Panel on Climate Change (IPCC).

IPCC (1992), Houghton, J.T., et al. (eds), *Climate Change 1992: The Supplementary Report to the IPCC Scientific Assessment*, Cambridge: Cambridge University Press for the Intergovernmental Panel on Climate Change (IPPC).

Lean, G. & Hinrichsen, D. (1992), *Atlas of the Environment*, Oxford: Helicon.

Seger, J. (1995), *The State of the Environment Atlas*, London: Penguin.

UN (1994 rev.) *Long-range World Population Projections, Two Centuries of Population Growth, 1950-2150*, New York: United Nations.

UNDP (1994 and other years), *Human Development Report*, New York & Oxford: Oxford University Press.

UNEP (1992), *One World, Environment and Development, 1972 to 1992*, Nairobi: United Nations Environment Programme.

UNESCO (1992), *Environment and Development Briefs*: *No.1 Debt for Nature*; *No.2 Ground Water*; *No.3 New Technologies*; *No.5 Disaster Reduction*; *No.6 Coasts*; *No.7 Biodiversity*, Paris: United Nations Educational, Scientific and Cultural Organization.

Wilson, E.O. (1988), *Biodiversity*, Washington, D.C.: Greenpeace International.

World Bank (1994), *World Debt Tables 1994-95*, two vols, Washington, D.C.: World Bank.

World Bank (1995), *Global Economic Prospects and the Developing Countries*, Washington, D.C.: World Bank.

World Bank (1995), *Social Indicators of Development*, Washington, D.C.: World Bank.

World Bank (1995), *The World Bank Atlas*, Washington, D.C.: World Bank.

World Bank (1995), *World Tables 1995*, Baltimore: The Johns Hopkins University Press.

WRI/UNEP/UNDP (1994), *World Resources 1994-95, A Report by the World Resources Institute in Collaboration with the United Nations Environment Programme and the United Nations Development Programme*, New York & Oxford: Oxford University Press.

Countries of the world

This map is for
identifying countries
only. The designations
employed do not imply
the expression of any
opinion whatsoever on
the part of the Food
and Agriculture
Organization of the
United Nations
concerning the legal
status of any country,
territory, city or area,
or of its authorities, or
concerning the
delimitation of its
frontiers or
boundaries.

COUNTRIES OF THE WORLD

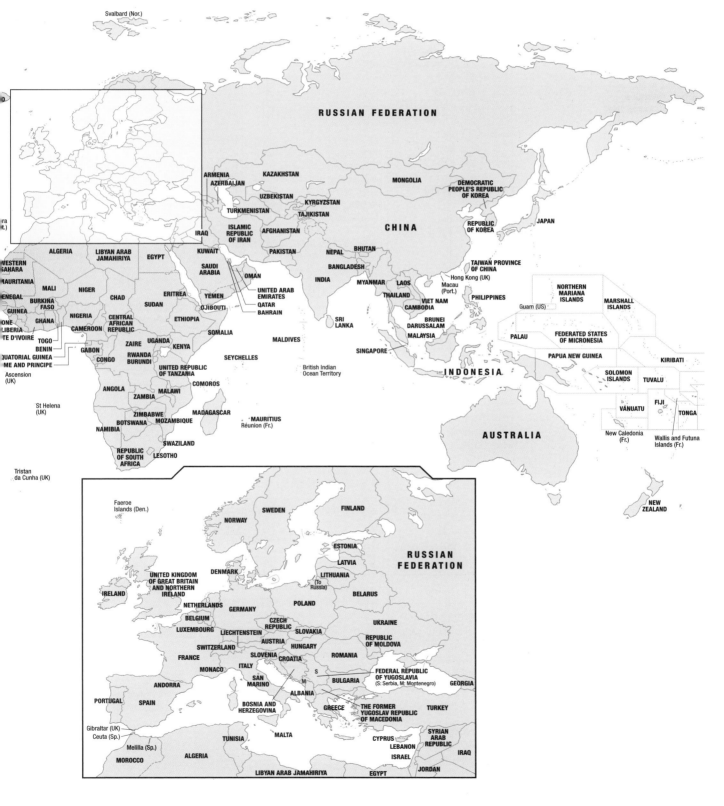

The United Nations system

UN Headquarters, New York. The UN is involved in every aspect of international life from peace-keeping to the environment, from children's rights to air safety, but it cannot legislate.

The United Nations (UN) is an organization of sovereign nations. It provides the machinery for its Member States to help solve disputes or problems, and deal with matters of concern to all humanity. It does not legislate.

The International Court of Justice (ICJ) is the principal judicial organ of the UN.

The General Assembly is the UN's main deliberative body. All Member States are represented in it and each has one vote.

The Economic and Social Council (ECOSOC) coordinates the economic and social work of the UN.

The Security Council has primary responsibility for maintenance of international peace and security. It has five permanent members each with the right to veto, and ten others elected for two-year terms. Member States are obligated to carry out its decisions.

The Secretariat services all organs of the UN except the ICJ, doing the day-to-day work of the UN, ranging from administering peace-keeping operations to organizing conferences.

The Secretary-General controls and directs the Secretariat, and is chief administrative officer at all meetings of the General Assembly, Security Council, ECOSOC and the Trusteeship Council.

The Trusteeship Council was established to ensure that governments responsible for administering Trust Territories took adequate steps to prepare them for self-government or independence. This task having been completed in 1994, the Council will now meet as and when required.

The specialized agencies and programmes have wide international responsibilities for development, health and economic, social, cultural, educational, scientific and technical, and other fields.

- ● Main and other sessional committees
- ● Standing committees and ad hoc bodies
- ● Other subsidiary organs and related bodies

- ▲ UNRWA United Nations Relief and Works Agency for Palestine Refugees in the Near East
- ▲ IAEA International Atomic Energy Agency

- ▲ INSTRAW International Research and Training Institute for the Advancement of Women
- ▲ UNCHS United Nations Centre for Human Settlements (Habitat)
- ▲ UNCTAD United Nations Conference on Trade and Development
- ▲ UNDCP United Nations International Drug Control Programme
- ▲ UNDP United Nations Development Programme
- ▲ UNEP United Nations Environment Programme
- ▲ UNFPA United Nations Population Fund
- ▲ UNHCR Office of the United Nations High Commissioner for Refugees
- ▲ UNICEF United Nations Children's Fund
- ▲ UNIFEM United Nations Development Fund for Women
- ▲ UNITAR United Nations Institute for Training and Research
- ▲ UNU United Nations University
- ▲ WFC World Food Council

- ▲ WFP World Food Programme
- ▲ ITC International Trade Centre UNCTAD/GATT

- ● FUNCTIONAL COMMISSIONS
  Commission for Social Development
  Commission on Crime Prevention and Criminal Justice
  Commission on Human Rights
  Commission on Narcotic Drugs
  Commission on Science and Technology for Development
  Commission on Sustainable Development
  Commission on the Status of Women
  Commission on Population and Development
  Statistical Commission

- ● REGIONAL COMMISSIONS
  Economic Commission for Africa (ECA)
  Economic Commission for Europe (ECE)
  Economic Commission for Latin America and the Caribbean (ECLAC)
  Economic and Social Commission for Asia and the Pacific (ESCAP)
  Economic and Social Commission for Western Asia (ESCWA)

- ● SESSIONAL AND STANDING COMMISSIONS

- ● EXPERT, AD HOC AND RELATED BODIES

Principal organs
of the United Nations

Security Council

- ● Military Staff Committee
- ● Standing committees and ad hoc bodies

Peace-keeping operations
- ▲ Various programmes

General Assembly

Economic and Social Council

- ■ ILO International Labour Organization
- ■ FAO Food and Agriculture Organization of the United Nations
- ■ UNESCO United Nations Educational, Scientific and Cultural Organization
- ■ WHO World Health Organization

International Court of Justice

World Bank Group
- ■ IBRD International Bank for Reconstruction and Development
- ■ IDA International Development Association
- ■ IFC International Finance Corporation
- ■ MIGA Multilateral Investment Guarantee Agency

Secretariat

- ■ IMF International Monetary Fund
- ■ ICAO International Civil Aviation Organization
- ■ UPU Universal Postal Union
- ■ ITU International Telecommunication Union
- ■ WMO World Meteorological Organization
- ■ IMO International Maritime Organization
- ■ WIPO World Intellectual Property Organization
- ■ IFAD International Fund for Agricultural Development
- ■ UNIDO United Nations Industrial Development Organization

Trusteeship Council

- ◆ WTO World Trade Organization

- ■ **FAO Food and Agriculture Organization of the United Nations**

Agriculture Department
  Animal Production and Animal Health
  Nuclear Techniques in Food and Agriculture (joint FAO/IAEA)
  Land and Water Development
  Plant Production and Protection
  Agricultural Support Systems

Economic and Social Department
  Agriculture and Economic Development
  Commodities and Trade
  Food and Nutrition
  Statistics

Fisheries Department
  Fishery Policy and Planning
  Fishery Resources
  Fishery Industries

Forestry Department
  Forestry Policy and Planning
  Forest Resources
  Forest Products

Sustainable Development Department
  Research, Extension and Training
  Women and People's Participation
  Rural Development and Agrarian Reform

Technical Cooperation Department
  Investment Centre
  Field Operations
  Policy Assistance

Regional (sub-regional) offices
  Africa (Southern and East Africa)
  Asia and the Pacific (the Pacific Islands)
  Latin America and the Caribbean (the Caribbean)
  The Near East (North Africa)
  Europe (Central and Eastern Europe)
Liaison offices
Representations in over 100 member nations

KEY:

- ▲ United Nations programmes and organs (representative list only)
- ■ Specialized agencies and other autonomous organizations within the system
- ● Other commissions, committees and ad hoc and related bodies
- ◆ Cooperative arrangements between the UN and the newly established WTO are currently under discussion

Photography credits

Page

12		N. Brodeur/WFP
14	top	E. Linusson/FAO
	bottom	G. Bizzarri/FAO
15		Dr R. Clark & M. Goff/Science Photo Library
16		F. Mattioli/FAO
18		T. Page/FAO
25		FAO
26	top	F. Mattioli/FAO
	left	P. Gigli/FAO
	bottom	A. Wolstad/FAO
27	top	J. Van Acker/FAO
	bottom left	A. Wolstad/FAO
	bottom right	T. Fenyes/FAO
28	main picture	E. Amalove/FAO
	left, from top	T. Kidd/Rex Features
		F. Botts/FAO
		R. Faidutti/FAO
29		J. Arboleda/FAO
30	top	A. Conti/FAO
	bottom	T. Fenyes/FAO
31	top	A. Wolstad/FAO
	bottom	J. Van Acker/FAO
32	top	H. Chazine/WFP
	bottom	P. Johnson/FAO
33	top	P. Johnson/FAO
	bottom	Jenny Matthews
35		K. Fennestad/FAO
38		F. Botts/FAO
39		L. Dematteis/FAO
42		M. Marzot/FAO
44	from top	R. Faidutti/FAO
		A. Conti/FAO
		FAO
45		A. Jensen/FAO
46		G. Bizzarri/FAO
49	left	R. Faidutti/FAO
	right, top	F. Paladini/FAO
	bottom	F. Paladini/FAO
56	left	S. Jayaraj/FAO
	main picture	F. Botts/FAO
57		P. Johnson/FAO
58	from top	S. Hannelius/FAO
		S. Murray/ Panos Pictures
		A. Evans/ Panos Pictures
		H. Wilson/ Panos Pictures
		J. Hartley/ Panos Pictures
60	from top	H. Them/ UNEP-Select
		R. Faidutti/FAO
		C. Mossop/FAO
		G. Bizzarri/FAO

62	left	T. Loftas
	right	M. Boulton/FAO
63	main picture	S. Nace/ Panos Pictures
	lower left	H. Null/FAO
	middle	M. Boulton/FAO
	bottom	T. Loftas
64	from top	FAO
		FAO
		G. Tortoli/FAO
		N. Cattlin/ Holt Studios
65		G. Tortoli/FAO
68	top	Seitre/BIOS
	bottom	Seitre/BIOS
69	top	E. Parker/ Still Pictures
	bottom	F. Gilson/BIOS
70		F. Mattioli/FAO
73		MS in Bodleian Library/Mary Evans Picture Library
76	top	C. Boscardi/FAO
	bottom	E. Kennedy/FAO
77	top	F. Mattioli/FAO
	bottom	A. Conti/FAO
78		J. Van Acker/FAO
79		G. Diana/FAO
82		P. Johnson/FAO
83		IAEA/FAO
84	left	F. Botts/FAO
	top right	F. Botts/FAO
	bottom right	IAEA/FAO
85		G. Diana/FAO
86	top left	F. Botts/FAO
	bottom right	V. Villalobos/FAO
87	panel, clockwise from left	P. Johnson/FAO
		IAEA/FAO
		S. Pierbattista/FAO
	far right	J.C. Revy/Science Photo Library
88	top: left, centre	F. Botts/FAO
		N. Cattlin/ Holt Studios
	bottom: left	I. de Borghegyi/FAO
	centre	C. Errath/FAO
89	right	IPGRI
	right	S. Pierbattista/FAO
90		FAO
91	main image	FAO
	left, from top	FAO
		FAO
		FAO
93	top	FAO
	middle	FAO
	bottom	R. Faidutti/FAO

95	right, top	D. Van Tran/FAO
	bottom	F. Botts/FAO
97		L. Dematteis/FAO
98		H. Wagner/FAO
100		FAO
102		R. Faidutti/FAO
104		R. Cannarsa/FAO
105		F. Mattioli/FAO
106		G. d'Onofrio/FAO
108		G. Bizzari/FAO
109	top	P. Johnson/FAO
	bottom	G. Bizzarri/FAO
110	top	M. Cherry/WFP
	bottom	R. Faidutti/FAO
111	top	G. Bizzarri/FAO
	bottom	A. Odoul/FAO
112	main picture	F. Mattioli/FAO
	left	G. Bizzarri/FAO
114		A. Zhigailov/ UNEP-Select
115		copyright The Nobel Foundation
116-7	clockwise from top left	A. Odoul/FAO
		P. Johnson/FAO
		G. Bizzarri/FAO
		T. Page/FAO
		F. Mattioli/FAO
		G. Bizzarri/FAO
		P. Johnson/FAO
		F. Botts/FAO
	centre	FAO
126		FAO